SUCH A DEATHLY DESIRE

SUNY SERIES IN CONTEMPORARY CONTINENTAL PHILOSOPHY

Dennis J. Schmidt, editor

SUCH A DEATHLY DESIRE

Un si funeste désir

PIERRE KLOSSOWSKI

Translated, Edited, and with an Afterword by

RUSSELL FORD

State University of New York Press

Un si funeste désir © Editions Gallimard, Paris, 1963.

Published by
State University of New York Press, Albany

© 2007 State University of New York

Printed in the United States of America

For information, contact State University of New York Press
www.sunypress.edu

Production and book design, Laurie Searl
Marketing, Michael Campochiaro

Library of Congress Cataloging-in-Publication Data

Klossowski, Pierre.
[Un si funeste désir. English]
Such a deathly desire / Pierre Klossowski ; translation and afterword by Russell Ford.
    p. cm. — (SUNY series in contemporary continental philosophy)
Includes bibliographical references and index.
ISBN 978-0-7914-7195-1 (hardcover : alk. paper) — ISBN 978-0-7914-7196-8 (pbk. : alk. paper) 1. French literature—20th century—History and criticism. 2. French literature—19th century—History and criticism. 3. Philosophy in literature. 4. Philosophy, Modern. I. Title.

PQ307.P47K56 2007
190—dc22

2006036600

10   9   8   7   6   5   4   3   2   1

Contents

Editor's Preface to the French Edition

Pierre Klossowski was born in Paris in 1905 to a family of Polish ancestry. His older brother was the painter Balthus; their father, Eric Klossowski, was a painter and art historian; their mother was a student of Pierre Bonnard.

The childhood and adolescence of the two brothers was spent amidst artists and writers. In their immediate circle, they had close relations with Rilke as well as Gide and these became determinants for the respective interests of the two boys: the friendship of Gide, who would take Pierre under his tutelage after the latter completed his secondary studies at Janson-de-Sailly, was especially important for him.

Daily contact with the author of *The Immoralist* caused a number of moral dilemmas for Pierre Klossowski that absorbed him for many years before they were resolved through the creation of an *oeuvre*.

In 1928, he collaborated with Pierre Jean Jouve in a translation of Hölderlin's *Poémes de la Folie*.

In 1935, after having frequented the circles of the Parisian Society of Psychoanalysis, whose *Review* published his first text on Sade, he met Georges Bataille with whom he formed a deep friendship that would last beyond the events of the war and until Bataille's death. It was at Bataille's prompting that Klossowski made contact with Breton and Maurice Heine, in the group *Contre-Attaque*, and, later, that he would participate in the Review *Acéphale* and meet André Masson.

During the Occupation, he began scholastic and theological studies with the Dominican faculty of Saint-Maximin, continued them in the Fourvière seminary at Lyon, and, finally, at the Catholic Institute in Paris. In Paris he was in contact with the Resistance networks. On the day after the Liberation, he collaborated in the ecumenical review *Dieu vivante*. However, he returned to lay life, married in 1947, and published a work that caused a sensation: *Sade mon prochain*.

His first novel, *La vocation suspendue*, published in 1950, is one of the transpositions of the vicissitudes of his religious crisis. But the most important part of his novelistic work is contained, on the one hand, in the trilogy of *Lois de l'hospitalité* [comprising *La révocation de l'Edit de Nantes* (1959), *Roberte ce soir* (1954), and *Le Souffleur* (1960)] and, on the other hand, in *Le Baphomet* (1965) which was awarded the *prix des Critiques*.

Pierre Klossowski further expressed himself in the essays *Le bain de Diane* (1957), *Un si funeste désir* (1963), and most importantly in an exegetical work: *Nietzsche et le cercle vicieux* (1969).

In cinema, he collaborated with Pierre Zucca in a film, *Roberte, ce soir*, as well as with Raul Ruiz in *L'Hypothèse du tableau volé* and *La vocation suspendue*.

For approximately the last twenty years, however, he has devoted himself almost exclusively to painting. Expositions of his work in France and abroad show that his reputation in this domain will only grow.

Translator's Note

Klossowski's style is infamously idiomatic. In 1965, the prominent critic and author Roger Caillois resigned from the jury of the literary *Prix des Critiques* over the awarding of that year's prize to Klossowski's novel *The Baphomet*. In his "denunciation" of Klossowski's novel, Caillois cited the pervasive stylistic and grammatical irregularities of the work as his reason for his abrupt and public disavowal. These irregularities are, however, not without reason, and one can observe in Klossowski's work, including the essays that compose the present volume, the use of multiple syntactic forms drawn from Latin, German, and archaic French.

This, of course, presents a problem not only for the reader but also for the translator. To try to mirror these diverse stylistic forms through some sort of system of "equivalent" English stylistic innovations seems to be a task alternately Herculean or Sisyphean. To simply pass them on to the English reader seems equally unjustifiable insofar as it would involve a willful blindness toward the situation of the work's original expression. Therefore the present translation has been produced with the primary aim of making the content of Klossowski's work available to an English audience while, at the same time, not entirely removing the stylistic strangeness of Klossowski's prose. This of course entails a certain interpretive prejudice regarding the themes of this work and the Translator's Afterword attempts to make this prejudice clear.

Because many of the people, places, and events cited by Klossowski may be unfamiliar to English readers, brief notes have been added where clarification seemed necessary or helpful. References to existing English translations of works cited by Klossowski have been cited wherever possible with occasional adjustments being made to fit Klossowski's own emphasis. References in Klossowski's text are formatted erratically—sometimes as footnotes, sometimes as in-text citations, sometimes absent entirely. All of these references have been rendered uniformly as footnotes.

Translator's Acknowledgments

This translation has accumulated a remarkable number of debts during its long—indeed overly long—gestation. Thanks is owed first of all to the fortuitous conjunction of *Toxicodendron rydbergii* and prednisone that generated the insomnia responsible for a draft translation of the final essay. Its initial anthropological debt is to Rich Doyle, who has been an enthusiastic supporter of this project from the very beginning.

Along the way, numerous people have contributed their expertise, advice, and insight into various aspects of translation as well as Klossowski's thought in general: Daw-Nay Evans, Ian James, Leonard Lawlor, Al Lingis, Bryan Lueck, Michael Naas, Jeff Nealon, Elizabeth Rottenberg, Alan Schrift, Charles Scott, Dan Smith, Allan Stoekl, and surely many others. Special thanks to Dan Smith, who read through a complete draft of the final essay, and to Bryan Lueck, who did the same for the remaining essays; both offered several helpful suggestions and the relative smoothness of the translation owes a great deal to their efforts. Any infelicities and errors that remain are the translator's alone.

Jennifer Paliatka of the A. C. Buehler Library at Elmhurst College, Sally Anderson of North Park University Library, and the assistants at the Newberry Library in Chicago provided technical assistance and helped in tracking down various references, both familiar and obscure.

Dennis Schmidt recognized the value of this work early on, and I am delighted that he found a place for it in his remarkable series. At SUNY Press, Jane Bunker has shown a great deal of kindness and demonstrated a truly superhuman degree of patience. I hope that this work does credit to them both.

Finally, although this is not my book and so a dedication seems impertinent, I would be remiss if I did not acknowledge the uncanny yet wonderful debt that I owe to Holly Moore, my Grace, who has endured quite a bit, but greeted it all with good cheer and encouragement.

Chapter One

On Some Fundamental Themes of
Nietzsche's *Gaya Scienza*

The name "Nietzsche" seems to be irredeemably associated with the notion of will to power, and not even so much with the notion of will as with the notion of power pure and simple. The most recent interpretation sees this as a sort of metaphysical commentary on the *fait accompli*, as a morality of conquest—and then everything else follows: the laboratories and their unspeakable experiments, the suppression of degenerates, foreigners, and the elderly, the crematory ovens, the criminals and the nuclear weapons; everything and everyone can now lay claim to the spirit of the father of modern immoralism: the typical *superman*[1] is a captain of industry, an explorer, a great cardiologist, chemist, engineer, a benefactor of humanity, passing as the product of the professor of "vital power." "Who then is Nietzsche?" ask the innocent, and the *Larousse* responds: *His aphorisms have had a great influence on the theoreticians of German racism.* In vain, it seems, in vain the 377th aphorism of the *Gaya Scienza* clamors with a distant, all-too-distant voice: *We who are homeless are too manifold and mixed racially in our descent, being "modern men," and consequently do not feel tempted to participate in the mendacious racial self-admiration and racial indecency that parades in Germany today as a sign of a German way of thinking and that is doubly false and obscene among the people of the "historical sense."*[2]

As this new edition of the *Gaya Scienza* is presented to the public—the third since those words first appeared in the French language—we ask ourselves whether, in light of recent events, it is appropriate to verify the enduring value of such a thought.[3] Certainly a spirit who single-handedly constitutes the silent demands of an age acquires more or less "importance" insofar as conventional wisdom attributes to him the inspiration for aberrant tendencies: the erroneous interpretation of the "overman," deliberately isolated

1

from its corollary, the doctrine of eternal return; the *death of God*, the *nothing is true, everything is permitted*—which has been a stale slogan in the ethical and social domain for the last half-century—this in the context of political machinations which, if one argued for the culpability of every word, spoken or written, would only ever be the inevitable ransom for a spiritual moment lived in the exclusive felicity of a soul carried to the point of incandescence; the retreat, the isolation, but also the compromising of a vision's unity, this is what would allow the appropriate extrication of the experience that bears the name of Nietzsche, both from its own historical context as well as the misappropriations to which it was fatally subjected by posterity.

The first words of the above-cited passage seem to define clearly the intelligible aspect of the first lesson to be drawn from this experience: "We who are homeless—as *modern* men—are too manifold and mixed." In its most everyday sense, as far as we are concerned, we who are reading it now. Too manifold and mixed, that is to say, too aligned with everything that has ever lived, fixed firmly in several places; in a word, too rich and hence too free to be forced to alienate this richness and freedom for a belonging concretely determined by space and time, and therefore having such a polyvalence of feeling that no undertaking limited to a concrete interest could exhaust our power of expenditure; this, according to Nietzsche, is what constitutes "modernity." But lest one misunderstand him: this is not a question of some vague cosmopolitanism; *modern* means a previously unattained aptitude for *sympathy* by virtue of which the mind enters into immediate contact not only with what seems to be the most foreign, but also with what was formerly the most bygone world, the most remote past. Conquest of a new possibility for living! *We homeless ones*; toward what *place* do they aspire, where then do they in fact live?

On the mountains, isolated, untimely, in past or future centuries;[4] and for Nietzsche this is the same thing: at the apex of knowledge, the mind demands for itself *every lived moment* of history, identifying the ego with history's different types as with so many versions of itself. Here the *vis contemplativa* will have been absorbed by will to power, for this will has no other goal than its innermost necessity: to reintegrate this universe which, in its multiplicity, wants to be and remain identical to itself.

In terms of its "modernity" the mind is in the same situation, the same exile of its will, that culminates in the adventure of knowledge lived by the "reborn" humanists, particularly the German humanists of the Reformation that *Faustus*, the *Fortunate* doctor—whose fortune is to *re-live* his life—famously incarnates. For these humanists nourished by the Platonic notion of recollection, knowledge [connaissance] of the past—co-nascence [co-naissance] in the past—which ought to deliver the secret of the future [l'a-venir], is doubled by the theological conflict of freedom and serfdom [serf-arbitre], of human freedom and divine grace, of damnation and election. IF I AM

ELECTED, EVERYTHING IS FORGIVEN IN ADVANCE. IF I AM DAMNED, EVERY-
THING IS STILL PERMITTED TO ME HERE BELOW. What's the difference? Eternity. *Mutatis mutandis*, for Nietzsche the atheist, inheritor of the simultaneously Protestant and Platonic humanist speculation (with its components:
nostalgia for Antiquity, attraction to the Roman world, contradictory
respect for the Neronian Papacy, "Caesar-Christ," etc.), *knowing whether the
knowledge of the past assures me eternity* remains the obscure theme of his
thought, verifiable on the different planes of both the philosophy of history
and the doctrine of the eternal return of an identical world. For Nietzsche
the "modern" world, with its social conflicts and its nihilistic morality of
progress, is only an interlude of shadows just as the Scholastic world was for
the humanists: it is on the other side of this interlude that the sun *to come*
[*à venir*] will rise from the *deciphered past*. The dilemma freedom—or serfdom? is transparent in the expressions: "will to power," "death of God,"
"nothing is true, everything is permitted," as is its resolution in the sense of
predestination. Such is the necessity of the eternal return (all is forgiven: the
ultimate meaning of Zarathustra's blessing). For humanism (Faust), knowledge, gnosis, finds itself under the sign of the Serpent which promises with
its polytheistic prediction: *eritis sicut dii*, the eternalization of man through
knowledge.[5] The day will come when the will of the "murderer of God" will
receive its pardon—that is to say when the Serpent will symbolize both the
forgetting of knowledge and the consummation of the eternal return of all
things. Damnation will come from this "historical sense" that overwhelms
modern man because he withdraws from the past, and thus from his original
possibilities, from his future; in other words damnation will come from the
nihilism *of the one who cannot pardon the crime of crimes*. And we will see that
to be *modern*, for Nietzsche, amounts to being set free, by the very knowledge of history, from the rectilinear progression of humanity—the irreversible "dialectical" march of historical materialism—in order to attempt to
live according to a representation of the *circle* where not only *is everything
forgiven*, but what's more *where everything is paid back*—where the notion of
grace is reintegrated with myth, even as the possibility of *myth* is confused
with *grace*.

I will now turn back to one of Nietzsche's texts that precedes the publication of *The Gay Science* by twenty years, the famous *Untimely Meditation* of
1876 entitled: *On the Advantages and Disadvantages of History for Life*, in order
to retrieve three key notions: the *instant*, *forgetting*, and the *will*, this triad out
of which it is precisely knowledge that will be born, and then we will perhaps
better understand how from the science of the past one comes, in the feeling
of the future, not merely to a knowledge, but to a *joyful knowledge* [*gai savoir*],
a *gaya scienza* that coincides with a recuperation of the past, but whose joy is
the rediscovery not of a properly historical past, but of the nonhistorical passage of the future in the past, of the present in the eternal.

The pretext for this *Untimely Meditation* of 1876 is the danger of the hypertrophy of the *historical sense*, and thus of the obsessive fear of the past, a specifically German problem, quite relative to the time; nevertheless what interests us here is the very paradoxical way in which Nietzsche is led from now on to develop his conception of existence—particularly to discredit the "historical sense" of the past—under the pretext of liberating the present from it, while it is apparently by a positive notion of *forgetting*—actually by an *unconscious* remembering—that he seeks to reestablish, on the plane of culture, an even more immediate contact with the most distant *past*. As a point of departure for this *Untimely* [*Meditation*] Nietzsche chooses the way that the instant is lived differently by the animal, the child, and the adult human being. If the animal, *who at once forgets and for whom every moment really dies, sinks back into night and fog and is extinguished for ever*,[6] suggests the first image of an *unhistorical* life, the child offers the adult the moving spectacle of a life that still has *nothing to repudiate*, because it *plays in blissful blindness between the hedges of past and future*.[7] For the adult, on the other hand, *a moment, now here and then gone, nothing before it came, again nothing after it has gone, nonetheless returns as a ghost and disturbs the peace of a later moment. A leaf flutters from the scroll of time, floats away—and suddenly floats back again and falls into the man's lap. Then the man says: "I remember."*[8] Torn away from the serene blindness of childhood that conceals forgetting, he comes to understand the phrase: *this was*, suitable for calling him back to what in fact constitutes his existence "an *imperfectum* that can never be perfected . . . and death at last brings the desired forgetting, by that act it at the same time extinguishes the present and all being and therewith sets the seal on the knowledge that being is only an uninterrupted *has-been*, a thing that lives by negating, consuming and contradicting itself."[9] This is a phrase that already contains and prepares Nietzsche's future and final doctrine in germinal form, as it is presented in the following proposition: "In the case of the smallest or of the greatest happiness, however, it is always the same thing that makes happiness happiness: the ability to forget or, expressed in more scholarly fashion, the capacity to feel *unhistorically* during its duration. *He who cannot sink down on the threshold of the moment and forget all the past, who cannot stand balanced like a goddess of victory on the threshold of the instant, on a single point, without growing dizzy and afraid, will never know what happiness is*—worse, he will never do anything to make others happy. . . . Forgetting is essential to action of any kind, just as not only light but darkness too is essential for the life of everything organic. . . . Thus: it is possible to live almost without memory, and to live happily moreover, as the animal demonstrates; but it is altogether impossible to live at all without forgetting."[10] And, in effect, when the will is liberated from the "historical sense," it will be identified with this very thing that lives only through its own contradiction; thus in the lived instant it is no longer identified as the ghost of a later instant, but as serenity, no longer blind, but ludic; the universe itself will no longer appear as an *imperfectum*, but rather will assume the characteristics of a *child that plays*. In sum:

"*There is a degree of sleeplessness, of rumination, of the historical sense, which is harmful and ultimately fatal to the living thing, whether this living thing be a man or a people or a culture. . . . To determine this degree . . . at which the past has to be forgotten . . . one would have to know exactly . . . what the* PLASTIC POWER *of a man, a people, a culture is: I mean by plastic power the capacity to develop out of oneself in one's own way, to transform and incorporate into oneself what is past and foreign.*"[11] There would thus be a way of existing both within and outside of history. As for a "historical sense" determined at one moment in history, it establishes a fallacious relation of the lived instant with both the historically reflected past and the time left to live; if it exalts the past, it empties the present; if it establishes the tasks for the present as following from those accomplished in the past, it dishonors the past as it reduces the fortunes of the present: for a state of consciousness does not allow one to judge what was previously accomplished in the unconscious, nor can someone ever act [*pas plus que l'homme ne saurait jamais agir*] in the present if he did not suspend the consciousness of his own past; and, in effect, what constitutes history are essentially acts or works of individuals who proceeded spontaneously by *blindness* or *injustice*, at the very moment that they created or acted, thus by *forgetting*; history is therefore composed exclusively of acts and creations that arise from forgetting, from whence follows a close relation between *forgetting* and the *creative will*. History actually teaches the contrary of what the "historical" mind projects into it: not a more and more conscious projection of man, but the uninterrupted return of the same inexhaustible dispositions through the course of successive generations; to understand history in this sense, counter to the science that proclaims its *fiat veritas pereat vita*,[12] is precisely to attain to a life *outside of history*, thanks to the impetus of the notion of return; *what was possible once ought to be possible once again* and far from finding in this a motive for idleness or sterility, man ought to begin for the sake of beginning; what he will have willed will have always been the accomplishment of what he thought he did not will, for since he did not escape from this existence by *consciously* wanting *to escape*, this existence wants to make him *forget the moment to come* in order to unerringly rediscover the integrity that characterizes every work or significant action [*action d'envergure*]. Here the *suprahistorical forces* par excellence are displayed, *art and religion which, diverting the glance from becoming, carries it to everything that gives existence an eternal character and an identical meaning. Science, which wants nothing to do with the eternal nor the existent, nothing except becoming, the historical,* can only detest art and religion—these *eternalizing* forces, these forces of *forgetting*—the very negation of science—in which past, present, and future are blended together.

This conception, at the antipodes of every philosophy of history that stems from Hegel, interests us here only to the extent that we can later see

Nietzsche, in his own case, capitalizing on this notion of a life outside of history, and confirming with his own life this thought counter to the historical current, ultimately finding there his own fatality. If the possibilities of departed humanity are always valid in every individual, at every instant of history, then for Nietzsche it is a matter of waging a merciless war against everything that wants to smother the *continually possible* in man: both in moral utilitarianism (which implies a mercantilism) and in that scientific organization of social life that the Hegelian heritage draws as a consequence of the agony of Christianity. On the other hand, because in our world Christianity itself is *a beautiful piece of the ancient world* for which it was the exit, lifting his gaze beyond two thousand years of Christian morality Nietzsche regards it as an access-way or path of return to Antiquity. Does he not say in another passage from that *Untimely Meditation* of 1876: *If we were really no more than the heirs of Antiquity . . . even if we ourselves decide to take it decidedly seriously in all its grandeur only in order to see in it our unique and characteristic privilege, yet we would nonetheless be obliged to ask whether it really was our eternal destiny to be pupils of* FADING ANTIQUITY: *at some time or other we might be permitted gradually to set our goal higher and more distant, some time or other we ought to be allowed to claim credit for having developed the spirit of the Alexandrian-Roman culture so nobly and fruitfully—among other means through our universal history—that we might now as a reward be permitted to set ourselves the even mightier task of striving to get behind and beyond this Alexandrian world, of aspiring to something more temporally remote in order to seek our models in the original ancient Greek world of greatness, naturalness and humanity. But there we also discover the reality of an essentially unhistorical culture and one which is nonetheless, or rather on that account, an inexpressibly richer and more vital culture.*[13] One finds in this passage Nietzsche's persistent nostalgia which, following Hölderlin, always opposed him to his age and that in fact inspires this anti-Hegelian and *suprahistorical* conception according to which the world, instead of marching toward some sort of final salvation, rediscovers itself at *each moment* of its history *fulfilled* and at its end. Thus *the past and the present are one, with all their diversity identical in all that is typical and, as the omnipresence of imperishable types, the universe is a motionless structure of a value that cannot alter and a significance that is always the same.*[14] First enunciated on the philological and historical plane of culture, this paradoxical attempt to live in the countercurrent of history by recuperating the most distant past through forgetting precipitates Nietzsche into his decisive experience. *The stronger the innermost roots of a man's nature, the more readily will he be able to assimilate and appropriate the things of the past, and the most powerful and tremendous nature would be characterized by the fact that it would know no boundary at all at which the historical sense began to overwhelm it; it would draw to itself and incorporate into itself all the past, its own and that most foreign to it, and as it were transform it into blood.*[15] Twenty years later the problem of the "historical sense" and of the life "outside of history" is so bound up with his own existence that he writes in *The Gay Science: Anyone who manages to experience the history of humanity as a whole as his own history will feel in an enormously generalized way all the grief of an invalid who thinks of health, of an old man who thinks of the dreams of his youth, of a lover deprived of his beloved, of the martyr whose ideal is perishing, of the hero on the evening after a battle that has decided nothing but brought him wounds and the loss of his friend. But if one endured, if one could endure this immense sum of grief of all kinds while yet being the hero who, as the second day of battle breaks, welcomes the dawn as his fortune, being a person whose horizon encompasses thousands of years past and future, being the heir of all the nobility of all past spirit—an heir with a sense of obligation, the most aristocratic of old nobles and at the same time the first of a new nobility—the like of which no age has yet seen or dreamed of; if one could burden one's soul with all of this—the oldest, the newest, the losses, hopes, conquests, and the victories of humanity; if one could finally contain all this in* One Soul *and condense it into a* Single Feeling—*this would surely have to result in a* happiness *that humanity has not yet known: the happiness of a god full of power and love, full of tears and laughter, a happiness that, like the sun in the evening, continually bestows its inexhaustible riches, pouring them into the sea, feeling richest, as the sun does, only when even the poorest fisherman is still rowing with golden oars! This godlike feeling would then be called—humaneness.*[i]

But this condensation of humanity that is bound up in a single soul can only be realized in the forgetting of a "historically" determined present, in a forgetting for the benefit of which the resources of the soul are liberated, resources that constitute its plastic force of assimilation; thus, in the project of a return toward the original world of ancient Greece, Nietzsche makes an appeal to "nonhistorical" images, subjacent to their rational elaborations, and thus to myth; this scholar, he for whom science has attained a *degree of insomnia*, attributes to *forgetting* the positive function of a *sub-coming [sous-venir]*[16] all the more fruitful since it is necessarily "untimely" [*inactuel*], all the more actualizing [*actualisant*] since it acts in the unconscious. One could speak here of lived "culture," but this term is only a mediocre translation of the troubling fate of the spirit that says to itself: I am many. The abundance of knowledge "converted into blood" increases along with the spiritual faculty of *being other*, which does not require an exclusive, normative truth: "It wasn't I! Not I! But a god through me." *The wonderful art and gift of creating gods previously coincided with a plurality of norms: one god was not considered a negation of some other god, nor blasphemy against him!;*[ii] perhaps the Serpent with its *sicut dii* insinuated this *greatest advantage of polytheism*. And to the extent that knowledge thereby develops the power of metamorphosis, a life lived once and for all

---

i. *The Gay Science*, Book 4, §337, pp. 268–269.
ii. *The Gay Science*, Book 3, §143 (Klossowski cites §141), p. 191.

suddenly appears more impoverished than a single instant rich with many ways of existing; this is why a single instant thus charged, thus sub-comed to [*sous-venu*] in the suspension of the consciousness of the present, suffices to reverse the course of a life. Hence the illuminative character of the *Gaya Scienza* whose many aphorisms testify to the moments of an ecstatic serenity: because from then on he had the feeling (formulated seven years later at the height of his madness) *that at bottom I am every name in history*,[17] of losing his own identity in the very certitude of finding it again, multiplied, in the identical permanence of the universe; it may be that similar instants are reserved to him precisely by virtue of their familiarity, intense to the point of strangeness, as the manifest proof of the cyclic nature of existence; thus he *sub-comed to* [*sous-vint*] what *is*-to-come for him, *sub-coming* [*sous-venu*] precisely in the *forgetting* of the coming moment. Similar moments are expressed in the following aphorism: *What would you say if some day or night a demon were to steal after you into your loneliest loneliness and say to you: "This life as you now live it and have lived it, you will have to live once more and innumerable times more; and there will be nothing new in it, but every pain and every joy and every thought and every sigh and everything unutterably small or great will have to return to you, all in the same succession and sequence—even this spider and this moonlight between the trees, and even this moment and I myself. The eternal hourglass is turned upside down again and again, and you with it, speck of dust!" Would you not throw yourself down and gnash your teeth and curse the demon who spoke thus? Or have you once experienced a tremendous moment when you would have answered him: "You are a god and never have I heard anything more divine." If this thought gained possession of you, it would change you as you are or perhaps crush you. The question in each and every thing, "Do you desire this once more and innumerable times more?" would lie upon your actions as the greatest weight. Or how well disposed would you have to become to yourself and to life to crave nothing more fervently than this ultimate eternal confirmation and seal?*[iii]

A passage which, in its parabolic form, is hardly capable of rational elucidation, because this is not its object: the eternal life that recovers *forgetting*. The ego grasps something here that it cannot be reminded of: that life that it has already lived innumerable times. If it has forgotten this life, that is because it has lived it in all of its details, which are exactly like those *here and now*. But, because the ego has lived it in an *identical* way, when it relives it again, there will be nothing new in it. And because of this, the ego will no longer be able to remember not only having already lived, but also having already willed—even though it *sub-comes* [*sous-venir*] to the very eternity of this willed life. And nevertheless the eternity of the will rises up here in the temporality of the instant like a new event—to answer the question: *Would*

---

iii. *The Gay Science*, Book 4, §341, pp. 273–274.

you will all of this once again?—and then the affirmative response bears "this eternal confirmation." But here again the demon's words raise the least interval up to the *"once and for all"*: in such a way that this question would also have been posed countless times. And because the eternity of the will is situated only beyond *Lethe*,[iv] and because one cannot both will again and be

---

iv. Because the eternal decision and the *choice of destiny* are made only on the other side of the *Lethe*, one does not know how to remember immediately, Plato would say here. And it seems that the parable of *the heaviest weight* here inverts and reflects, like a mirror, the essential scene of the *choice of destiny* by the souls of the deceased at the threshold of their reincarnation, as it is depicted in the *myth of Er* in the Tenth Book of Plato's *Republic*: at the end of a cycle of a thousand years, passed either in celestial beatitudes or in infernal expiations, according to their merits, the souls of the deceased are instructed to choose a new destiny and in order to do that are reassembled before the three Fates, Lachesis, Clotho, and Atropos, daughters of Necessity and weavers of the destinies of which each one sings: Lachesis the *past*, Clotho the *present*, Atropos the *future*; but, for the deceased there is first "an immediate obligation" to go before Lachesis—thus toward the Fate that figures the past, for it is in the past—on the knees of Lachesis—that the lots are drawn that correspond to the types of existences that may be chosen: *"This is the speech of Necessity's maiden daughter, Lachesis*. Souls that live a day, this is the beginning of another death–bringing cycle for the mortal race. A demon will not select you, but you will choose a demon. Let him who gets the first lot make the first choice of a life to which he will be bound by necessity. . . . The blame belongs to him who chooses; god is blameless.'" "He said that this surely was a sight worth seeing: how each of the several souls chose a life. For it was pitiable, laughable, and wonderful to see. For the most part the choice was made according to the habituation of their former life." (This is precisely the: *Would you will all of this once again?* of the Nietzschean parable!). . . . "When all the souls had chosen lives, in the same order as the lots they had drawn, they went forward to Lachesis. And she sent with each the demon he had chosen as a guardian of the life and a fulfiller of what was chosen. The demon first led the soul to Clotho—under her hand as it turned the whirling spindle—thereby ratifying the fate it had drawn and chosen. After touching her, he next led it to the spinning of Atropos, thus making the threads irreversible. And from there, without turning around, they went under Necessity's throne. And, having come out through it, when the others had also come through, all made their way through terrible stifling heat to the plain of Lethe ("Forgetting"). For it was barren of trees and all that naturally grows on earth. Then they made their camp, for evening was coming on, by the river of Amelēs ("carelessness") whose water no vessel can contain. Now it was a necessity for all to drink a certain measure of the water, but those who were not saved by prudence drank more than the measure. As he drank, each forgot everything. When they had gone to sleep and it was midnight, there came thunder and an earthquake; and they were suddenly carried from there, each in a different way, up to their birth, shooting like stars." Plato, *Republic*, 2nd Edition, trans. Allan Bloom (New York: Basic Books, 1991), pp. 300, 302–303. [Klossowski cites from the French translation by Léon Robin.]

This myth—quite familiar to Nietzsche—would in this sense clarify his notion of forgetting, more specifically the parable of the *heaviest weight* that, in the necessity of freely willing the eternal return, we must find again *hic et nunc*—like recrossing the *Lethe*—the moment of the choice of our destiny, made outside of present time ("outside of history"),

already living, the parable of *the heaviest weight* is presented to the understanding as an *aporia*: if one sees here only the coincidence of extreme despair
and extreme hope, the ultimate curse and blessing, the vertigo of existence
overcoming the mind, as the mind recovers the extreme point of vertigo, following the example of "*a goddess of victory on the threshold of the instant, on a
single point, growing neither dizzy nor afraid*" whose image it projects; as principle of every event, it [the eternity of the will] creates out of this very vertigo
to which it attains and that it in some way conquers; and ultimately, when it
speaks a sentence exclusive of every creation: *there will be nothing new in this
relived life*, it forms, in order to conform to it, the image of this demon that
reveals to it its law, the image of the hourglass in which it is reversed . . . for
the mind identifying itself in its eternity with the law of the temporal circle
where the past and the present necessarily coincide, turns back upon itself in
the instant, but as the imperative question that its own eternity addresses to
it: by virtue of which the ego, as a willing and responsible being, finds itself
instructed to fulfill its destiny as if it were *not already* fulfilled by the sole fact
of existing; if I do not freely choose the reiteration (seemingly incomprehensible and absurd) of my actions that are already accomplished many times
over, I will have ceased to be myself as master of my own secret, as an incar-
nation of this sovereign law, without however ceasing to act necessarily as its
supreme confirmation: I can only be myself by freely willing my necessarily
relived life. But the law of the eternal return abolishes the dilemma at the very
moment that it poses it again: not responsible for being reiterated, lost, and
immediately found again, the ego at each moment again becomes responsible
for willing itself again as it has necessarily always been and necessarily always
will be—its free decision will never have exhausted the eternity of its being
whose circular movement will always bring back the imperative: *Will yourself!*
in order to abolish the moment to come. And nevertheless the question that
everything poses to the subject: *Would you still will all of this innumerable times?*
must be answered by me, insofar as I am an other; for by virtue of this over-
whelming law, I no longer resent *gravity*, I attach less importance to the pre-
tence for my actions, I no longer take my own casualness seriously. . . . In this
way the eternalization of the ego, in which the aspiration to eternity wants
itself to be explained by a cyclical conception of being, amounts to rationalizing an ecstatic instant inexplicable by nature which, in itself, eliminates
through the identification of lived time with eternity every other communicable expression except the image of the circle: a late fragment composed dur-

---

guided by our "Demon." For in order to have drunk only "moderately" from the water of
the river "Amelēs," both the faculty of "recollection" that grounds re-cognition and also
the anxiousness for willing the accomplishment of this "new" destiny—for Nietzsche, the
same—are required of us.

ing the time of the *Revaluation of All Values* (1885) says it again: "in effect will-ing the universe *such as it was and such as it is, re-willing it, for ever, for eternity, shouting insatiably* DA CAPO—*not only to himself but to the whole play and specta-cle, and not only to a spectacle but at bottom to him who needs precisely this specta-cle—and who makes it necessary because again and again he needs himself—and makes himself necessary—What? Wouldn't this be—*CIRCULUS VITIOSUS DEUS?"[v]

When the spectacle of the surf at the edge of the sea shows him in the eager movement of the waves—filled with the lust for *buried treasures*—the very nature of the will as his own secret: *Thus live waves—thus live we who will!* was this very secret not in the "*as if it were a question of attaining something!*" whereas here is nothing but this eager movement, nothing but this lust for buried trea-sures; in effect nothing but this *will to collect oneself* in the coming and going of the waves: the soul regains sovereignty over itself precisely through the procla-mation of a law of the identical return of all things; it is seen here living out-side of history in the fabulous society of waves: *Dance as you like, roaring with overweening pleasure and malice—or dive again, pouring your emeralds down into the deepest depths, and throw your infinite white mane of foam and spray over them: Everything suits me, for everything suits you so well, and I am so well disposed toward you for everything; how could I think of betraying you? For—mark my word!—I know you and your secret, I know your kind! You and I—are we not of one kind?— You and I—do we not have one secret?*[vi] And this secret—the very lesson of the *Gaya Scienza*—is that this glorification of motion for motion's sake destroys the notion of any sort of end of existence and exalts the useless presence of being in the absence of every end: an error of pretexts by virtue of which life "wills the misery of lived being," the human species declines, but "the instinct for conservation" always creates something out of it appropriate to the preserva-tion of the vertigo of being, to the anguish of an existence without purpose; but if pretexts have always functioned to hide the uselessness of existence (*as though it were a question of achieving something*), only religious symbols as well as artis-tic simulacra could explain man's adherence to the *uselessness* of being.

The greatest recent event, he says at the beginning of the Fifth Book of the *Gay Science*—that "*God is dead,*" *that the belief in the Christian God has become unbelievable—is already beginning to cast its first shadows over Europe. For the few at least, whose eyes—the suspicion in whose eyes is strong and subtle enough for this spectacle, some sun seems to have set and some ancient and profound trust has been turned into doubt; to them our old world must appear daily more like evening, more mistrustful, stranger, "older." But in essence one can say: The event itself is far too great, too distant, too remote from the multitude's capacity for comprehen-sion even for the tidings of it to be thought of as having arrived as yet. Much less*

---

v. Cf. *Beyond Good and Evil*, III, §56.

vi. *The Gay Science*, Book 4, §310, pp. 247–248, translation modified.

may one suppose that many people know as yet what this event really means—and how much must collapse now that this faith has been undermined because it was built upon this faith, propped up by it, grown into it; for example, the whole of our European morality.[18] And further on: As we thus reject the Christian interpretation and condemn its "meaning" as counterfeit, SCHOPENHAUER's question immediately comes to us in a terrifying way: DOES EXISTENCE HAVE ANY MEANING AT ALL? It will require a few centuries before this question can even be heard completely and in its full depth.[vii] Nevertheless it is in the death of God, the event of events, proven in the parable of the Madman to be the crime of crimes, that the decisive moment of the will comes to be situated in the circular necessity of being; there on the contrary the event in some way emerges from forgetting as a rewilled action: for men this deed is still more distant from them than the most distant stars—AND YET THEY HAVE DONE IT THEMSELVES![viii] And so for Nietzsche, nihilism, following upon the historical situation of the "agony of Christianity," can only be overcome by taking account of the will as a sacrilegious act: God is dead . . . and we have killed him! . . . What was holiest and mightiest of all that the world has yet owned has bled to death under our knives: who will wash this blood from our hands? What water is there for us to clean ourselves? What festivals of atonement, what sacred games shall we have to invent?[19] The notion of overhumanity means nothing if one isolates it from the context in which nihilism must be taken as sacrilege: the overman announces itself as a new maturity of the spirit returned to the without possible end where the fall outside of the human and the flight beyond seem to coincide, they are indiscernibles; it is even unclear what the fact of the will should resolve and surpass. The freedom where the murderer of God finds himself again (moral nihilism), because it follows from the suppression of the Decalogue (of the you ought), is immediately reversed into a necessary blindness where the ego survives only if something is imposed upon it again: you ought, the you ought to will.—Will what? Will nothingness? The simple situation of the West's fate: unconsciously willing, because humanity does not know how to will nothing for the sake of nothing, while it abandons itself to nothingness in its powerlessness to will. (And Nietzsche, who elsewhere denounces the mystique of nothingness, speaks here of the wretched nooks and crannies where our most intelligent contemporaries energetically lose themselves, in the petty aesthetic creeds, such as Parisian naturalism . . . or in nihilism, following the St. Petersburg model, meaning the belief in unbelief even to the point of martyrdom.[ix] On the other hand he sees the consequences of nihilism in the general feeling of emptiness and its compensation, the need for excitement, that characterize

vii. Ibid., §357, p. 308, translation modified.
viii. The Gay Science, Book 3, §125, p. 182, translation modified.
ix. The Gay Science, Book 5, §347, pp. 288–289, translation modified.

the modern world.) The reaction that Nietzsche is trying to formulate against nihilism, after having raised it to the conscious formulation of a historical situation, finds its motivating force not only in the notion of *death*, but in the *putting to death* of God, as a sacrificial act of a sacrilegious will, from the moment that the will rediscovers the integrity of being as a reintegration of its sovereignty; it is by acquiescing to the very movement that carries the ego to the deepest pit (where the death of God and deicide merge) and that brings it back to the highest summit that the will is affirmed in an ultimate act, in the moment when the *you must will*, passing into a *willing itself as itself*, attains to: *I am as I always was and always will be*. But this reintegration of the sovereignty of being in the statement *I am* is not conceived here in the sense of an accidental ego who utters it to the exclusion of everything else, like that of Max Stirner, the post-Hegelian who proclaimed the pure and simple assumption of nothingness by the ego proper: *I have based my cause upon nothing*.[20] Thus if Nietzsche wants to give to the nihilism of fate, to vulgar atheism, the pathetic tone of the deicide proclaimed by the *Madman*, he is not trying to promote nothing for the sake of nothing, nor negation for the sake of negation, but rather the acquiescence to being that the moral God of Christianity, according to him, granted only to a utilitarian alienation, an alienation of the richness of existence by morality (for Nietzsche synonymous with greed); and the destruction of the Christian morality has as its goal not license in the sense given it by vulgar atheism, the rejection of Christianity does not aim to overcome a religion of suffering with a passion for existence, but through a negotiation where passion, reduced to pain, reclaims salvation as the only misery. *We are, in a word—and let this be our word of honor!*—GOOD EUROPEANS, *the heirs of Europe, the rich, overjoyed, but also overly obligated heirs of thousands of years of European spirit. As such, we have also outgrown Christianity and are averse to it—precisely because we have grown out of it, because our ancestors were Christians who in their Christianity were uncompromisingly upright: for their faith they willingly sacrificed possessions and position, blood and fatherland. We—do the same. For what? For our unbelief? For every kind of unbelief? No, you know better than that, friends! The hidden* YES *in you is stronger than all* NOS *and* MAYBES *that afflict you and your age like a disease; and when you have to embark on the sea, you emigrants, you, too, are compelled to this by—a* FAITH!*[21]

If, for Nietzsche, the notion of God "consolidates all the hatreds that have ever been directed against life," the overman, in the parables of Zarathustra, reintegrates the sovereignty of being with the divine only in the mythic sense, thus renewing the myth of an ancient divinity as well as a divinity to come: Dionysus, supreme figure of unceasing possibility, who, through Dionysian *pessimism*, will free man from his present nihilism.[x]

---

x. Ibid., §370, pp. 327–331.

4

 SUCH A DEATHLY DESIRE

To what extent can this doctrine be taught? Is it even communicable? To whom could it be? To whom is it addressed today? To whom? Or are these questions already out-of-date? This doctrine is not at all separate from his life, which, in our modern world, attempts to renew the ancient meaning of *fatum*: *I am a destiny.*[22] It remains to be seen whether the *amor fati*, a *"willed" fatum*, is not precisely the paradox of the modern consciousness that has "reintegrated" it by "interiorizing" it, the *Edict of Lachesis*.[xi] This willed *fatum* is incommunicable, inalienable precisely in its "alienation" in the pathological sense of the term. Ever since Nietzsche, for whom this was the only possible "modern" version of the *Empedoclean* descent into *Etna*, "mental alienation" has become part of the career of some men of letters and willed indiscretion is thereby subordinated to commercial vulgarization. Today a poet already knows that, if he becomes mad, his sanctification is assured. He knows in advance that: *a few thousand years more on the path of the last century!—and the highest intelligence will be manifest in everything that man will do: but precisely the kind of intelligence that is completely stripped of its dignity. It will certainly be necessary to be intelligent, but it will also be so ordinary that a more noble taste will experience this necessity as a* VUL-GARITY. *And just as a tyranny of truth and science is capable of highly esteeming a lie, so a tyranny of the intelligence is capable of producing a new type of noble sense. To be noble, perhaps that means: to be mad.*[23] Because it is situated at the decisive turning point of Nietzsche's life, it is fitting that the *Gaya Scienza* contains several considerations regarding the communicability of his experiences. Nietzsche had a nostalgia for disciples and perhaps also for an active, but closed, community. He always dreamed of a grand action, of social upheavals or disruptions of political institutions (did he not at Turin, swept along in the first fevers of madness, that is to say at the height of lucidity, having become at once *Dionysus* and *the Crucified*, want to convene the sovereigns of Europe in Rome in order to shoot the young Kaiser and the anti-Semites?).[24] And, to the extent that he estimated the possibility of an understanding, of an affinity with others, he also set forth the infallible law of the depreciation of a rare and authentic experience as soon as it enters into the habitude of a number of minds—to the point that it becomes the slogan of the fool, of a mass that appropriates it without passing through the torments, through the pains and the rightly inalienable fortunes of a solitary man. Gide's statement, "because he had to become mad, we can no longer become so,"[25] is true only if one draws a *practical* lesson from his teaching and particularly from his "immoralism." But regarding this relation, depreciation has done its work by way of industrial standardization. If there is a lesson that the reading of Nietzsche provides to every attentive reader, it is the horror of futility, and today immorality and futility are synonyms. The *old women, the white geese that have received nothing but innocence*

---

xi. Cf. note iv.

from nature, with which Nietzsche identifies the right-thinkers of his age, have dropped out of sight. One would almost love for them to return! The *tempting woman is a rare bird.* This sign of the times would change Nietzsche's optics. I note this in passing in order to recall the confusion, around 1900, between "Nietzscheanism" and the emancipation of women, the suffragette movement, the feminism in which he saw a symptom of decadence. Within the perspective of ascendant nihilism (in particular, the socialization, the massive proletarianization brought about by the industrial world with its excessive production, its cult of productivity for the sake of productivity—all conditions of a generalized demoralization), Nietzsche foresaw two movements that he placed in his own personal context, the climate of the "death of God." *Two movements are then possible; one is absolute: a leveling of humanity, great anthills, etc.; the other movement, my own: which, on the contrary, will accentuate all the antagonisms, all the intervals—a suppression of equality, which will constitute the task of superpowerful men. The first movement engenders the type of the* LAST MAN, *my own movement that of the overman. Its goal is absolutely not to conceive or to institute this category like the teachers of the preceding, but rather to make the two categories coexist:* SEPARATED *as much as possible—one hardly caring about the other like the Epicurean gods.*[xii] I am emphasizing the last phrase here in order to indicate clearly that every idea of an "ideological" organization exercising power is opposed to his aspirations which are here of a utopian order. Thus it is still interesting to sketch what he thought of the chances for a closed community. *Whenever the reformation of a whole people fails and it is only sects that elevate their leader, we may conclude that the people has become relatively heterogeneous and has begun to move away from rude herd instincts and the morality of mores: they are hovering in an interesting intermediate position that is usually dismissed as a mere decay of morals and corruption, although in fact it proclaims that the egg is approaching maturity and that the eggshell is about to be broken. . . . The more general and unconditional the influence of an individual or the idea of an individual can be, the more homogeneous and the lower must the mass be that is influenced, while countermovements give evidence of counterneeds that also want to be satisfied and recognized. Conversely, we may always infer that a civilization is really superior when powerful and domineering natures have little influence and create only sects. This applies also to the various arts and the field of knowledge. Where someone rules, there are masses; and where we find masses we also find a need to be enslaved. Where men are enslaved, there are few individuals, and these are opposed by herd instincts and conscience.*[xiii] The *Gaya*

---

xii. cf. *The Will to Power* [This passage comes from the *Nachlass* material, but is not included in the English edition of *Will to Power*. Friedrich Nietzsche, *Sämtliche Werke: Kritische Studienausgabe*, ed. Giorgio Colli and Mazzino Montinari, Vol. 10 (Berlin: Walter de Gruyter, 1980), pp. 244–245, 7[21], Spring–Summer, 1883.—trans.]

xiii. *The Gay Science*, Book 3, §149, pp. 195–196.

Scienza, fruit of the greatest imaginable solitude, speaks essentially to those spirits who, themselves, have *found* this solitude *again*, thus to those natures that a
depth of nobility disposes to refuse *distraction* and *work at any price*, thus to bear
l'ennui: here we touch upon the resources of solitude, which, despite his
extreme isolation, gave him the feeling of always being "among us" [*entre nous*].
*Whatever in nature and in history is of my own kind, speaks to me, spurs me on, and
comforts me; the rest I do not hear or forget right away. We are always in our own
company.*[xiv] Regarding *states of elevation*, it seems to him, he says, that most people hardly believe in the reality of such states of the soul, except those who
know firsthand an extended state of elevation [*un état d'élévation de longue
durée*]. He adds that the fate of the individual being who incarnates a unique
state of elevation has until then hardly been an *elevating possibility*, but that one
day it could happen that history will bring forth such men, *once a great many
favorable preconditions have been created and determined that even the dice throws of
the luckiest chance could not bring together today. What has so far entered our souls
only now and then as an exception that made us shudder might perhaps be the usual
state for these future souls: a perpetual movement between high and low, the feeling
of high and low, a continual ascent as on stairs and at the same time a sense of rest-
ing on clouds.*[26] Is it not striking that he awaits from history, that is to say from
human evolution, the creation of these "preconditions" by virtue of which the
exceptional state of the soul would become an *ordinary* state? Is he not saying
here that these so-endowed future souls would be every soul? But even when he
imagined here an elect few—indeed a quasi-"priestly" class—he who so
strongly appreciates the laws of Manu—knowing that these prerequisite conditions are created in the ascetic field proper to religious communities, he
nonetheless seems to have foreseen, again, that his own privileged instants—
the feeling of *an incessant movement between the high and the low*—lead to his
own living conditions, his solitude, that never escapes the inexorable law of depreciation [*dé-préciation*]. That is to say: the expropriation of a personal case,
which necessarily accompanies the creation of prerequisite conditions which
are accessible to many, and soon to everyone; unless a superior "new spirituality" is attained by the entire human species. Either case confirms the eternal
return that implies the abolition of every personal life returned to being, for the
greater glory of being.

---

xiv. Ibid., §166, p. 200.

Chapter Two

Gide, Du Bos, and the Demon

Anyone who dares to study Gide in terms of the demonic must begin by asking himself what the terms "demon" and "demonic" mean. The makeshift [*improvisé*] exorcist, circumscribing the demon under the pretext of clarifying a case as complex as Gide's, kills two birds with one stone: if by chance Gide manages to escape from this procedure, it is because the Devil has carried him away. *Pereat Gide, fiat Diabolus.*[1] A man can honestly believe in God without believing in the Devil, can believe in the Devil without believing in God, and can admit the demonic without believing in either one. Catholic dogma affirms that only God is existence and that the Devil, as Devil, is nothing and that he exists as pure spirit only by having received being like every other creature; a created spirit, he reveals his demonic tendency by his contradictory aspiration to be in order to cease to be, to be in order not to be at all, to be by not being. From the Scholastics' point of view, Satan committed an ontological error: he believed being could be conceived as evil, as nonbeing, and having thus revolted against the principle of contradiction he waited for Hegel to destroy it. And we see that Du Bos will bring a similar grievance against Gide for *evading the principle of contradiction and for involving himself with these combined fragments that constitute the fact of believing in the demon and believing in nothing at all.* A bizarre reproach. In effect, by virtue of this ontological definition that is not exactly that of the Gospel (*You cannot serve two masters*), the demon could not be one of the two simultaneous postulates that Baudelaire speaks of, because it cannot be the pole opposed to God unless it is also his existence.[2] Since it denies being, the demonic spirit must borrow a being other than its own; being itself only pure negation, it needs another existence in order to exercise its negation. It can only do so through creatures, who lack being through themselves but have instead received it. The spirit seeks to associate itself with creatures in order to know its own contradiction, its own existence in the nonexistent. In this regard, if one goes back to the Church Fathers, and thus to a tradition not yet embarrassed by Aristotelian quibbles, one finds in the demonology of Tertullian, for example, a much more sober and precise definition and, regarding our subject, some particularly clarifying images. For Tertullian, the demon is essentially the simulator; certainly it gives form to desires in dreams and in spectacles, but more than anything else it simulates the dead in order to substantiate the preexistence of the soul and its wandering on the surface of the earth and thereby to discredit the dogma of the resurrection of the flesh.[3] Such, in broad strokes, is the traditional idea of the demon; lacking its own personality, it is prior to every inclination, every influence, owing to its borrowed existence. It is immediately apparent how the resulting ontological argumentation can be applied to both the immanent and the transcendent plane, winding up with a value judgment that favors transcendence. If, rejecting all metaphysics, being is no longer distinguished from concrete reality, and what belongs to it from what falls purely and simply under sense, then everything that is spiritual, according to the traditional distinction between being and the existent, could be judged diabolical—according to the sort of reason that only learns the lessons of concrete reality—insofar as the spiritual would want to turn man away from the experience of the concrete. On the other hand, the sort of reason that can deliver the spirit of man from the habits of the spirit would truly be the savior. Fear of the concrete would then be inspired only by the Devil and the temptation would be to try to flee from experience. The identification of God with being, and of the demon with nonbeing, is a rough translation of common sense onto the plane of reality, and immediately provides an account of the morality of "good sense": transcendence in its totality, everything that is given as transcendent or supernatural, is to be blamed on the wicked power. Is it a question here of an inversion as claimed by Du Bos, who, according to Gide, wants to see a substitution of Satan for God? Absolutely not; for on this basis of concrete experience, which is also Tertullian's, the temptation of the spirit is always the same: either to deny what is there, or to affirm what is not there. To succumb to the Devil is to succumb to deception. And this is indeed Gide's position; whatever reveals [découvrir] is of God, whatever prevents discovery [découverte] is of the Devil; here again the terms God and Devil have a character that is only natural. His effort consists not only in demonstrating that there is no point whatever in denying their content, but also, as far as he is concerned, in pronouncing them. If it is still sometimes expressed in traditional terms, this is because both believers and unbelievers know quite well what the terms God or Devil mean; more so than the terms Good and Evil, these names, because they are names, describe the aim of an orientation that does not belong so much to concrete experience as to the consciousness of what a fulfilled experience leaves subsisting in the spirit. Perhaps it is because Gide, feigning nonexistence, has seen the height of the simulacrum of the demon (You know quite well that I don't *exist*)[4]—which is in fact a way of simulating scholasticism—that Du Bos reproaches Gide for evading the principle of contradiction and for getting lost on the ontological plane when the problem is a moral one; but, because Gide never forgets that art is a simulacrum, the artist a simulator, specifically the one who exhausts language; by choosing the *name* of the Devil, Gide is poured out [*Gide s'est plu*][5] in translating the ambiguity of the problem of freedom by the ambiguous means of art. The *need* to do something is felt as an *instigation* as soon as the preliminary deliberation is supplanted by the act itself; in order to prevail over my judgment, perhaps my will has given way to something more powerful than myself so that I agree to will; the result, then, is that my freedom returns as servitude. Because it was a question of doing good or evil to be decided according to the judgment of value when the experience began, if I stop myself, I will collide with something more powerful than myself, with the feeling of having squandered an opportunity. If I do not stop myself, I will be submitted to an array of previously unsuspected rules. Am I responsible for my failure? Has *no one* prevented me in advance? But *who* has prevented me, *who* has urged me to disregard a command? If I am successful, what does that prove? Was the warning false? How then can one fail to listen to the voice: *Begin again and you will know if I was wrong. But if I was right, it is useless for you to say that you will obey me from now on, since you have already begun again.* Such are, roughly, the two sides of the *Devil* and *God* in the Gidean consciousness. Let us state it succinctly: it is the problem of arbitrary freedom, or arbitrary slavery, *deliberately restored to the level of a worldly lesson* [*leçon du choses*]. By having completely failed to discern this level that determines the term *demon* for Gide, the perspective of his research is distorted and the figurative expression that Gide intentionally borrows from the Gospel is confused with the supernatural world that the Gospel proclaims. But the Gospel supposes a nature preliminary to the *supernatural*, a worldly lesson preliminary to the spiritual lesson. If from the orthodox point of view Gide was wrong for not limiting himself only to the worldly lesson, he is none the less evangelical.

If there is nothing demonic about Gide's attitude (because the demon was only made in the *arid places* where Gide wanted it to be [*se voudrait*]), then on the contrary it becomes the object of preoccupation for another spirit, for the stronger reason of a spirit who, wanting to turn him toward itself, wants him to turn back against himself; the "demonic" intervenes immediately, the malicious fluidity (in Gide's sense as in the other's) establishes itself, motivating forces of self-love come into play; it is veiled to him, and the other who wanted him to conform to his own procedure, far from revealing it, obscures it. What's more, everything that the other zealously, carefully, contributes will only harden him and make him more opaque; the approach of a spirit who moves with the current that Gide has devoted all of his forces to

moving against, mobilizes in Gide a defense mechanism that will end up throw-
ing the other off, while he himself leaves him grappling with a sort of *duplicate*
of his person; what still lives in him, confused with his substance, detaches from
him like a piece of a false Gide that the other will contemplate, horrified; he
thinks that he is holding a living Gide, but between his hands there is only a
mannequin whose inanimate features bear an expression of mockery. This mannequin is the *demonic Gide* of the powerless converters, while the authentic
Gide, continuing to live, continues to remain ungraspable because he is alive.
There is certainly something sinister about this affair; at least this is how it
appears in the relations between Du Bos and Gide, but it only appears so—perhaps it was sinister for Du Bos. To judge by the disagreeable remarks made by
Gide *in petto*, this affair was only a comedy for Gide, or (if one takes account of
the illness that, during this period, befell both Gide and Du Bos in the course
of the elaboration of the *Dialogue*) some labored imbroglio that he turned into
comedy. This comedy could only be sinister for Du Bos. But he had to live his
part as infinitely serious, both for his own sake and apparently, in his eyes, for
Gide's. Now this gravity is precisely what is lacking in Du Bos's *Journals*; one
cannot help but say to each phrase: This will to seriousness and profundity
reveals a powerlessness to experience the serious and the profound. It is Du
Bos's very expression that is at issue here; such syntax betrays a *mania* for the
objects of his reflection, and especially for religious problems. The form that his
reflection affected for years, a form that couldn't be more pathological, that
extraordinary prolixity that creates so many subjects to indefinitely retain and
manipulate—as many subjects as words—a profusion of *entia rationis*, can only
veil the true crisis that he underwent while in contact with Gide; certainly he
evokes this crisis in places, but he does not establish its connection with his
concern for converting Gide. Madame Van Rysselberghe's statement to Gide,
reported by him in his own *Journal: He is gaining his salvation upon your back,*[6]
gives only one side of the inextricable situation within which Du Bos had
enclosed himself. It was not a question of his gaining salvation, but rather of
putting his own faith to the test "on Gide's back."

On the day after his conversion, Charles Du Bos knew the necessity, felt
by more than one neophyte, of *encountering the demon.* "What makes me still
completely lacking is the interior state that would provide the tone that I
want in order to attain the theme of the demon . . . I am at a turning point
where I want to deprive myself, once and for all, of this entirely intellectual
tone of argumentation, which is too much the tone of "reasoning" [*l'avoir raison*], and rejoin an emotional level that would bear me up to the final shore.
It is surely impossible to truly speak of the demon at the level of pure argumentation."[i] This same need seems to sharpen the taste for God; it testifies in

---

i. Charles Du Bos, *Journal intime*, v. 4 (Paris: Correa, 1950), p. 72.

certain temperaments to the dissatisfaction with which their commerce with divine realities leaves them. More than one page of the *Journal* recounts that, for Charles Du Bos, these realities belonged to the domain of sensible experience, and that religious life—rather than the emancipation of the aesthete's *jouissance*—is the supreme object of this *jouissance*. *Value, depth,* and *quality*— in Du Bos these terms designate elements of an affective atmosphere, and the pursuit of this atmosphere, from his youth up to the time [*l'époque*] of his *Dialogue with Andre Gide*, through all sorts of material and physical annoyances, constitutes the true preoccupation, the vital ground of his interior life or, better, of his *interior time*, his *lived time*. Du Bos evokes Proust in a number of ways—except that of a creative genius—and calls himself *a Christian Proust*. But nothing is so jarring as the coupling of this name and this qualifier. When he observes, in *If the Seed Should Die*, the absence of *influx* [*afflux*], *of the resurfacing of memory*, in Gide as opposed to Proust, he defines a characteristic of his own apprehension of things and beings: the resurfacing of memory is constitutive of the atmosphere in which Du Bos could not breathe. Thus his own religious experiences, such as those he describes in the *Journal* of 1928, are, under the guise of spiritual problems, objects of a morose delight; ultimately, if one compares them to the evocations from the time of his engagement and marriage (around 1907–1908) with which the *Journal* of 1928 begins, particularly to the spicy descriptions of the tea salons, of the racks of parasols and umbrellas, or of the séances of the manicurist de Z, the descriptions that he gives during 1928—of his masses, reflections, and elevations—one can't help being embarrassed that, for example, the description of the umbrellas—or of any other past object evoked—is situated on the same plane as the description of the masses, of the communions that he began to participate in and that he set himself to *reliving* almost immediately in his *Journal* under the pretext of deepening them. But where the *resurfacing of memory* supplants the greatest religious act, the nostalgia of the *Christian Proust* betrays its absurdity; for if it is always legitimate to recall what must melt away in everyday life, it is completely contradictory to recall what, by definition, does not belong to the everyday. Only someone who has lived in the sanctuary needs to recreate the sanctuary's ambiance—not the rupture between the here-below and the beyond so much as the accessories, the rites, and the attitudes that should produce this rupture. Ultimately these are the rites and attitudes that, when they become the objects of a retrospective evocation, come to the foreground and maintain the place of rupture, even when their evocation has prevented it. If, on the other hand, the everyday can serve to explain eternal life, treating the figures of eternal life as so many objects in themselves, by constantly going back to this in a *Journal* where ultimately one practices contemplating oneself under the pretext of contemplating the Lord, this amounts to something much less innocent than being quaintly disturbed at remembering some parasols that one gave to one's fiancée, of a shade chosen to match her

dresses. If consciousness works to hollow out an interior life from emotions
more or less strongly experienced in the course of a low mass, it always ends
up confusing the diverse *Stimmungen* with hearing the speech of a God who
has never cared much for incense—literally as well as figuratively. Charles Du
Bos's spiritual atmosphere is so *incensed* at this point that if the smell of sulfur did not intervene, it would not be religious at all, and faith would have no
object other than what Du Bos himself calls the *aesthetic miracle*. Fortunately,
someone providentially disperses this smell of sulfur, providentially and also
involuntarily: Gide again assumes the role of the diabolic thurifer.

All things considered, what is the *demonic* for Du Bos, and how can he
turn it into a positive notion to counter Gidean negativism? The conversations with Peter Wust, the German theologian and philosopher, that took
place around this time, were of some use,[7] but so were his own states of dry-
ness that he complains about, his own illnesses such as those that arise in him
from an incompatibility between spiritual responsibility and a sort of flight
into work, or the overriding necessity of reconciling the act of faith (which
has nothing in it of the creator) with aesthetic creation, impeded by devo-
tional obedience; all this will lead him to adopt a Goethean notion of the *daimon*, and to distinguish it from what he believes Gide's *demonic* to be: the
abandon to the pure demonic that he will identify as a defect due to the *insufficiency of being*. If he says that, even at the time of his unbelief, he never
stopped believing in original sin, this was in terms of a feeling of deficiency.
Because of this deficiency, temptation doesn't intervene under the guise of
obscure instinctive impulses, but rather through the action of the wicked
spirit upon a man's spirit; and because it thus attacks our consciousness, not
our instinctive nature, it acts through ideas, not our impulses: according to
Gide's own definition, the demon is above all an autonomous power. But, Du
Bos adds, "it is both interior and exterior to us. The Christian notion of the
homo duplex represents nothing other than the moment of coexistence of the
demon and the individual being." And if Gide says that the demon requires
a *reciprocal activity* from us, Du Bos claims that strictly speaking there is no
longer a double man, but a manipulated man. In his eyes, Gide is already a
manipulated man, but he does not grasp the idea that he himself is a manipulated man in Gide's eyes.

According to Du Bos, the best way to exorcise Gide would be to instruct
him to expose himself once and for all: "We know that you excel in eluding
the principle of contradiction, but *truly we cannot let you continue* to question
the combined fragments that constitute the fact of believing in the demon
and believing in nothing at all." It thus seems as though this is what the
"deepest" Gide believes and that his "rationalism is only the fruit of human
politeness." Because it has taken years for Du Bos to free himself from this
apparent rationalism, he does not despair of freeing Gide in turn. Under the
relation of the demon, Gide has effectively given some reassuring proofs of

his "concrete and antiphilosophical spirit," because he has affirmed the Devil's reality as that of a being, not that of a simple principle. Thus he acquires his fundamental antirationalism. Du Bos seems to base his hopes and his image of Gide on the image that the latter has of the Devil. Thus from this image, one that nevertheless carries no proof at all of Gide's antirationalism, Du Bos reproaches Gide using Baudelaire, since Gide never tires of citing the Baudelairean text on the *two simultaneous postulates*; Du Bos supposes that Baudelaire and Gide infer "an aesthetic value from the existence of Satan, a value that counterbalances God, almost equal to Him"; if, in Baudelaire, the case is more complex, then according to Gide there is an aggravating circumstance in every case that decides in Satan's favor. The God of Gide's pious adolescence becomes a pure abstraction, and Satan thereby becomes more concrete. Gide has knowingly or unknowingly confused the *Christian demon* with the Greek *daimon* (complicating the latter with the Goethean *dämonische*), a confusion that causes him to make the aesthetic operation consist of an *abandon to the pure demonic*. This sophism is expressed in *If the Seed Should Die*: "And I then came to doubt if God even required such constraints, if it was not impious to ceaselessly rebel, and if this was not counter to him; if, in this battle in which I divided myself, I reasonably ought to place blame on the other." Identifying God with emancipation and Satan with servitude to the law—an interpretation that places Gide in the company of very old examples—Gide, according to Du Bos, by an "incomparable sleight-of-hand," has grounded "the two postulates in one," leading to a pure and simple deification of Satan himself. It thus seems that "the divine possibilities in him are stronger in the satanic direction." Because, in his *Dostoevsky*,[8] he insisted on the fact that for the Russian novelist all the demonic characters are intellectuals, this satanic inclination would be manifest in the temptation to sin against the Spirit: "Gide is a treasonous spiritual person."

Does this not give the impression that, in order to study Gide's case from the angle of the demon, and thus of nonexistence, Du Bos lets Gide escape just when he thinks he seizes hold of the demon, and that the demon vanishes when he is on the verge of seizing Gide? Is it not a question of defining the *nonexistence* of the Devil through Gide's concrete existence, in order to prove the *existence of nonbeing*; or, on the contrary, of defining *Gide's reality* through the *existence of nonbeing* in order to prove the nonbeing of existence, thereby striking a blow against Gide's reality? In both cases, Du Bos, for his part, evades the principle of contradiction, and therefore attributes a content to Gide's terms that they do not have. Du Bos thinks that he has clarified them by discovering the confusion between the Goethean and the Christian meaning of the Gidean term *demonic*; in doing so he forgets that he himself introduced an anti-Christian value by reconciling faith and the creative act, and that Gide, on the contrary, follows the most ancient Christian tradition when he emphasizes the collaboration of the demon in every work of art. If

Gide is deliberately equivocal in this regard, then Goethe is equally so. It is true that Goethe said to Eckermann that his own Mephistopheles was not endowed with the *dämonische*, because it is too negative; but a Mephistophelean element—*Schadenfreude*, the pleasure of injuring—nonetheless remains in Goethe's positive formulation of the demonic in *Dichtung and Wahrheit* [*Poetry and Truth*].[9] When Du Bos immediately takes the Gidean definition of the demon in a transcendent, supernatural sense, he thinks that by deliberately using the traditional term, Gide is departing from psychology, from the immanent, in order thereby to provide a guarantee of his Christian faith, an opportunity for those who might want to restore him to orthodoxy. But, if this were the case, Gide would be putting the principle of his own procedure back into question, including his definition of the demon. His deliberate use of this consecrated term only further emphasizes his own experience, whether as the cohabitation of contradictory or antagonistic personalities within a single individual, or as the exteriorization of one of these personalities due to an influence that affects one or that one exercises. To admit that contestation takes the form of a character who inhabits us almost to the point of making us complicit with our adversary does not thereby imply belief in a supernatural reality. When Du Bos, after having finally understood Gide's *identification of the demon* in his own way, comes to see in the *absence of a spontaneous sentiment for life* in Gide the favorable terrain for the influence of the demon on Gide's mind—an unexpected compensation, since Du Bos understands this lack of spontaneity to be nothing other than pederasty—it is apparent that Du Bos is trapped in a vicious circle. He began by admitting that Gide knew perfectly well how to identify the Devil and then wound up refusing Gide any power of discernment because he is a pederast. Thus from two things, one results: either the Devil can employ Gide's pederasty in such a way that the author of *Corydon*, because he won't give up his opinion, remains incapable of recognizing and identifying him, and in this case, it isn't necessary to depart from the supposition that *the deepest Gide believes*; or, on the contrary, if Gide's identification of the demon is legitimate, then this is because he was not hindered by pederasty, and in that case pederasty[ii] is nei-

---

ii. Thus, again, the cause is the pederastic reflexes in the Western world, by virtue of the clandestine conditions that have constituted it, the subterfuges, the evasions that characterize every wrongly or rationally oppressed social group; not an insufficiency of being but the inferiority complex with its compensations that affect a class psychologically, constituted through a millenary moral and social oppression, and which, nevertheless, is only a remnant of anachronistic sensibility from the point of view of the life of societies. On the one hand, Gide aspires to an order of disparate structures, to the heart of the post-Christian world, which, built by this order upon contrary laws, is in its turn at the point of being ruined by its own contradictions—contradictions of a world that Gide, on the other hand, is, by his formation, so allied to that he works with the post-Christian criteria to reestab-

ther an insufficiency of being, nor a lack of spontaneity that lends itself to
diabolic influence; and if he is even able to present the aspect of an *abandon
to the pure demonic*, how brilliant is the *confusion* or rather the *equivocation*
that Gide deliberately puts in these terms! For if it seems to him to have the
positive virtue of the *dämonische* defined by Goethe, which, as Du Bos
repeats, is not satanic in the Christian sense, Gide is too well versed with the
metamorphoses of the Devil to place any trust in such a flattering—because
also unilateral—definition of the *demonic*.

It is true that on two occasions Gide wrote that once he had admitted
"the existence" of the demon, the whole meaning of his life was clarified.[10]
But examining these texts closely, one notices that only one thing is in question: whether he is fooled by his own rationalizations in the course of dialogues improvised within his heart of hearts. The pact with the Devil is never
envisaged there, and if it remained a myth for Gide, that is because one does
not make a pact with a part of oneself, with one's double. On the other hand,
according to Gide the Devil is an agent of redoubling. This is well known to
Gide thanks to the Other having borrowed, in its nonexistence, the existence
of a Claudel, of a Charles Du Bos; the more ruptures there are with them, the
more ruptures there are with everything that, in him, prevented him from
finding himself.

---

lish the vanished structures of pedagogical pederasty in the relations of the master and the
disciple. In those relations it was an aspect of the search for truth. A vanished or hidden
order, the *Eros paidikos* becomes in the soul of a Gide, at the heart of all the moral and cultural circumstances that this name represents, both the nostalgia for an order and the principle of reflective dissociation; the dissolvent reflection of a hostile milieu, and the impetus for a personal destiny conditioned by the effects of this milieu. An inadequation of
means and ends thus arises for Gide; while the means tend to reconstitute a relational order
for which the conditions were previously lacking—since the *Socratic pederasty* is dead and
properly utopian—these means belong to a world that repudiates this pederasty, and the
result is the provocation of situations only ever lived as moments of a personal destiny—a
destiny that has no reference at all other than its own authority. Thus arises the inevitable
misunderstanding of those who judge Gide in the name of the means that he employs, and
their insistence on the perverted character of these means.

Chapter Three

In the Margin of the Correspondence
Between Gide and Claudel

On the eve of a meeting with Claudel from which he will come away with nothing more than another motive to be silent, Gide wrote to the poet: "Every day I mean to write to you, and then I draw back before the enormity of all that I could tell you."[i] Obviously, says the reader, who hoped to grasp the enigma's key. Considering the present state of this correspondence, disfigured as it is by unfortunate lacunae, Gide's retreat where one would expect the deferment of a confession perhaps gives a very precise meaning to "enormity." Everything in the surviving letters up until what we find in the one dated March 7, 1914, appears to revolve around this "enormity" of everything that Gide wanted to say, and thus they seem merely to express postponements, while Claudel's letters show the Catholic poet becoming lost on the false trails that Gide, for his part, has suggested to him as a plan [*dessein*]. How is it not obvious that this inequality of "exchanges," despite the gravity of the questions posed, despite the sincere tone, is actually a game of dupes—every time that we read the reflections that Gide noted in the interval in his *Journal*, that Mallet invites us to read and that he has, perhaps too ingeniously, judged necessary in order to fill in the lacunae left by Gide's vanished letters? The reader will not only read the passages of the *Journal* picked out by Mallet, he will refer to others, contemporaneous with the nagging questions of this correspondence, and, in the resulting context, will Gide not come to appear more equivocal than he really was? Certainly the man who writes to himself always does so in a manner different from that with which he addresses himself to others, even when he says the same things and when he

---

i. *The Correspondence Between Paul Claudel and André Gide*, Letter of December 17, 1905 (50/13).

is completely sincere in both cases. But a new and much more general question emerges from this doubt.

To what extent was Gide able to put into action a plan that was held in abeyance since the beginning of his career? Was there premeditation? Does this premeditation suppose some whispering demon [*démon souffleur*] that he employed and that, conversely, uses his inner destiny in order to exert an influence, perhaps even a similar premeditation, that it alone knows? For if we must take Gide at his word when, on various occasions, he affirms in his *Journal* that he carried his different works inside of himself at the same time—namely, *The Immoralist, Strait Is the Gate, The Caves of the Vatican*—and that only the material impossibility of writing them simultaneously obliged him to publish them successively, even if that meant giving the impression of a spirit subject to oscillatory movements—then one must recognize that, insofar as any project always supposes some unpreventable accidents, his meeting with Claudel put the execution of his program to singular test and that he overcame this meeting only through a no less singular attitude. Either the affirmation of the coexistence of the works is only a retrospective interpretation—and then the letters to Claudel, which more or less concern conversion, would testify to a true inner perplexity—or the coexistence of the written works also corresponds to some already intimately resolved problems, and then the tone of perplexity in these letters—which have quite unfortunately been destroyed by someone—only establishes a screen behind which Gide intends to preserve his freedom of action. Let us say that if we are inclined to believe this, we nevertheless do not think that things are so simple. But the more one compares the texts of these letters with the passages of Gide's *Journal* cited by Mallet, and above all with those that he does not cite at all, the less one can prevent the impression that, in this battle against a friendship that constantly threatened prematurely to discover the secret goal toward which he was headed, Gide can be seen developing a subtle game and pushing just far enough to avoid accentuating certain traits of his physiognomy.

There are two problems that already seem resolved for Gide at the moment when, corresponding with Claudel, the latter undertakes to convert him to Catholicism. The digression entitled *Christian Ethics*, from around 1900, offers an almost definitive representation of Christ the "emancipator," which he will maintain throughout his entire career. "We shall soon come, I believe, to isolate the words of Christ in order to let them appear more emancipatory than they had hitherto seemed. Less buried, they will appear more dramatically, *finally negating the institution of the family* (and *that will serve as authority for suppressing it*), taking man himself out of his environment for a personal career and teaching him by his example and his voice not to have any possessions on the earth or any place to lay one's head. Ah, my whole soul longs for that "nomadic state" in which man, without hearth or home, will no more localize his duty or his affection than his happiness on such creatures."¹ He then cites the words of Christ that, according to him, abolish the family, marriage, and even familial mourning ("Let the dead bury their dead") and he concludes by repeating Christ's warning: I am come to place division between a man and his father, between daughter and mother, etc., with this cry of exaltation: "Endless broadening of the object of love as soon as the family is negated."² This image of Christ, isolated from its traditional and Judaic context, extracted from the sacred history that constitutes the economy of revelation, as questionable as it is from a historical point of view, nevertheless has an authentic aspect even from the orthodox point of view, since it is precisely upon these words that the structure of the Church and the monastic orders is raised. One can never underestimate the importance of this interpretation of the Gospel for Gide's thought; it has nothing to do with liberal Protestantism, nor even with the seeming Quietism that Claudel at first thought he found in it. Gide's image of Christ, which connects more closely with that of Blake, will exempt him from creating a Zarathustra. And forty years after the aforementioned text, Gide inserts these pages into his *Journal*, where he declares that the teaching of Christ contains more emancipatory force, more abnegation and joy, than that of Nietzsche: "What am I saying: as much? I discover still more, and a more profound and more secret opposition; more assured and, hence, calmer."ⁱⁱ

Regarding the second problem, that of homosexuality, Gide judges that it is posed to him simply as a dilemma: to be or not to be, and, deciding to live, Gide has thus resolved it practically. But morally? Not by a long shot. So without maintaining that his homosexual tendencies contributed to the formation of his interpretation of Christ's antifamilial words, let us say that his way of understanding the Gospel remains a function of his self-given mission: to give a "moral and social" solution to the problem of homosexuality. When he meets Claudel, he had only given it a *pathetic* expression in *Saul* and *The Immoralist*, because he was preserving the norms of traditional consciousness. But he had already devoted a didactic work (*Corydon*) to it, which Claudel completely ignores, along with the presence and preoccupations that hold sway there in Gide's already consolidated spirit, even when they have both come to the threshold of intimacy. Claudel certainly seems the more eager of the two to surmount the problem. But at this point of mutual esteem, one has the impression that Gide's sympathy comes to a halt while Claudel explores the problem [*tandis que Claudel le tâte*]. He cares about Gide's soul. "Although it has not pleased God to make me one of His priests, I have a profound love

ii. *André Gide, Journals, Volume 3, 1928–1939,* trans. Justin O'Brien (Chicago: University of Illinois Press, 1949), p. 370, detached page from 1937.

of souls. Yours is very dear to me. Why can I not help you a little?"[iii] And Gide
says to him, moved: "No, I did not understand—how could I understand?—
that you had "a profound love of souls"? That was what I needed you to tell
me—and that my own soul was dear to you. You mustn't see it as a matter of
pride—but a hideous need of affection, of love, so great a thirst for sympathy
that I feared I was deceiving myself, and was only trying to draw near to God
in order to draw near to you—near enough, at any rate, to hear you better."[3]
And taking Claudel at his word, he expects that he in turn will understand
his own distaste for a practical and temperate religion, and that after having
drawn daily nourishment from reading the Bible in his youth, he has preferred "to break abruptly with my first beliefs rather than to arrive at some
lukewarm compromise between art and religion. Perhaps Catholicism would
have offered a less strenuous opposition within me—not so much to two
beliefs as to two systems of ethics. . . . *For the first time* the day before yester-
day (but I could glimpse it already in your books) I could see by the light of
your mind, not so much a solution—it would be absurd to hope for that—as
a new, and acceptable battleground. And do you know what was tormenting
me at this time—the difficulty, the impossibility perhaps, of reaching sanctity
by the road of paganism; and when you spoke to me, Claudel, of one's
"absolute duty to be a saint," did you guess that you could not have said anything to which I should react more violently? Ah! How right I was to be
apprehensive of meeting you! And how frightened I am of your violence at
this moment!"[4] What was this acceptable battleground? That of Christ
against the Churches? And is it not a question of a sanctity that would provoke Claudel's violence even more, of a sanctity that Gide is aiming at here
more rigorously?

One day Claudel writes to Gide that he has several excellent friends
among the Jews, Protestants, and atheists, such as Schwob, Suarès, and
Berthelot, but they are purely passive unbelievers and not personal enemies
of Christ.[iv] What Claudel is actually trying to uncover about Gide's case is
whether he too is one of these passive unbelievers who is waiting for someone to take him "under his wing," and Gide, whether willingly or unwillingly,
seems to fall under this illusion for a long time, since in December of 1911,
he confesses to Claudel that the reasons that keep him from renouncing
Protestantism are affective (a frequent argument among Protestants): "imag-

iii. *The Correspondence Between Paul Claudel and André Gide*, letter dated 12/05/05
(45–46/10).

iv. Ibid., letter dated 02/06/08 (70/32). [Marcel Schwob (1867–1905) was a symbolist
prose poet. André Suarès (1868–1948) was a French poet and essayist famous for his atheism. Philippe Berthelot (1866–1934) was the son of a well-known diplomat, Marcellin
Berthelot, who, like his father, entered into politics and served in the Ministry of Foreign
Affairs for many years.]

ine what it is like to have been surrounded in childhood with admirable and saintly people whom I love, in death as in life, whom I revere, and who *watch over me*, as you were saying. Jammes talks of my heredity; I let him have his say; but I can very well tell *you* that the secret of my incapacity to believe does not lie there (my brain is made up of almost as many Catholic as Protestant cells, after all); it lies rather in the fidelity which I owe to those people, my relations and my seniors, who lived in such constant, noble, and radiant communion with God, and gave me my noblest images of abnegation."[v]

In other exchanges Claudel wants to have a rational discussion with Gide about the articles of the Christian faith. First he submitted to him a notebook of citations taken from Scripture and the Church Fathers.[vi] On another occasion, he sent him a synopsis of the Christian doctrine that he composed for the benefit of a friend;[vii] later he sent him an extract from Chesterton's *Orthodoxy*.[viii] And we know that in 1912 Claudel again suggested to Gide that he give a formal account of his objections.[5]

Why doesn't Claudel ever obtain any overt reaction whatsoever from Gide when he puts him on the same plane as the dogmatist? Because Gide is, by his nature, impermeable to this form of thought—one wonders whether, despite his prodigious erudition and his perpetual reading of Bossuet's *Variations*,[6] he ever understood the doctrinal problems at the very heart of Protestantism that placed Calvin and Luther against each other— and simultaneously escapes both the doctrinal arguments and, even more, the Scholastic concepts that form Claudel's intellectual framework. Thus, even later, he will claim not to understand at all the poet's statement that "*evil does not compose*."[7] To the extent that Claudel's temperament finds its architecture in medieval ontology, even to the point of describing the modern world as would a man of the Middle Ages, Gide's temperament shows itself to be just as resistant in the face of any construction of thought except those that arise from art. Thus he resists any sort of metaphysics, which he clearly confuses with mysticism, since both are, for him, only pure mystification, whereas the ontological terms, emptied of meaning for him, ought to work to explain dogma. This is less a question of a natural phobia than of a

---

v. Ibid., letter dated 12/10/11 (170/124). [Francis Jammes (1868–1938) was a French poet who converted to Catholicism in 1905.]

vi. Ibid., letter dated 12/05/05 (45–46/10).

vii. Ibid., letter dated 03/03/08 (71–73/33).

viii. Ibid., letter dated 07/08/09 (94–97/50–51). [G. K. Chesterton (1874–1936) was a well-known and prolific English writer who converted to Catholicism in 1922. *Orthodoxy: The Romance of Faith* was published in 1908 as a companion to *Heretics* (1905). In *Heretics*, Chesterton critiqued a number of "heretical" thinkers and writers of the time, such as Kipling, Shaw, and Wells. In *Orthodoxy*, Chesterton set out to explain what made orthodox Catholicism persuasive to him.]

kind of circumcision of the heart—a mistrust in the face of his own affectivity—that reason dictates to his will. If then he deliberately encloses himself within the limits of common sense, this is because he has determined
that the economy of "sane" reason is as inexhaustible as the economy of
existence. Bound to this most mundane notion of reason, Gide neglects the
contradictions that reason implies. He seems never to have observed that
adherence to faith as the renouncement of reason to its own exercise is itself
one rational act among others. On the other hand, he never seems to ask
himself if reason ultimately wouldn't be just one form of pathos among others. These are some considerations that would be relevant to a study of
Gide's notion of reason. While a thought, oriented according to dogma, will
seek in life the signs that this thought refers to images given to it by dogma,
Gide forms a specifically iconoclastic psychology by pretending to do something else, only to then describe and comprehend the most disconcerting
motives of the soul according to the most sober good sense. And if for him
the representation of a world transcending reason nonetheless reacts upon
life and opens a field of experiences [ouvre un champ d'expériences]—an
unsuspected reaction for those who seek to understand existence only
through life itself—Gide describes and analyzes only in order to live more,
and lives only to understand even better, by the very fact of having simply
lived life. For Gide, turning the mind against life amounts to "losing" one's
mind, while "to lose one's life, is to become truly alive." The function of life
supposes, on the contrary, such a constant appeal to thought that Gide can
say to its spiritualist critics: there is no danger of sinning against the spirit
here at all, but the more one risks oneself in all of life's tests—the supreme
test consisting perhaps in choosing life when the heart requires death—the
more one also requires of life, because there is never as much life—which
fears the possibility of damnation—as reason, always unsatisfied, requires. A
long time after his debate with Claudel, Gide commended subterfuge as a
supreme virtue in his Theseus; at the antipodes of the propter vitam, vivendi
perdere causas,[8] life has no other reason to be except life. Rejecting the
dogma and figures of religious language, secularizing the Gospel, Gide easily
assumes the habits of a "naturalist" and he only awaits the single experience
of life as his reason for being, not as the revelation of a truth. He pleads for
his sensibility as though for a completely unperverted aspect, authentically
part of the natural economy, and this preoccupation later comes to be more
and more confused with retaining a respectful expression before common
sense. For if common sense rejects what has seemed contrary to him for a
long time, it is by his own means that he allows this annoyance to be less-
ened. Gide shows that this "common sense" is often only an alleviation of
reason by lengthy habituation to the "reasons of the heart." This is doubtless
what explains Gide's return to a rationalism that often shows no fear of
appearing as a perfect, but always deliberate, platitude. At the time of his

dialogues with Claudel, Gide's artistic fecundity was still nourished by his ambiguity; between the necessity of saying certain things and the implicit prohibition in the language that he nevertheless had to express them in, they could still only be produced as masked. Whence the misunderstanding [malentendu] in the exchanges with Claudel, where it is ultimately a matter of a wicked insinuation [mal sous-entendu].

Because of his dogmatic indifference, Gide met Claudel's advances and interventions with a beautiful mask [beau jeu face]; his secret dispositions always allowed him to shy away from Claudel, as well as from his own conscience whenever it seemed ready to give in to the "batterings" of the Catholic poet. If Gide was a poor Calvinist, comfortable with his own orthodoxy, with a few regrets about his forbidden sensibility, perhaps he would join the converter's game. But Gide is only vaguely a Protestant; he owed to it no more than a few atavisms and reflexes. These gave him a suspicious mind— in terms of himself and others; externally, he distrusted influential or persuasive behaviors (in this case the Catholic apology and casuistry), internally, he distrusted his own sensibility, his impulses. Gide had the sort of mind that by "defying his nature" with his marriage, he constituted a censure within his own thought. This is a most serious censure, because this responsibility for affection before someone cherished will remain irreconcilable with Gide's responsibility toward his own thought. This gives rise to a battle against Protestant morality and its own discriminatory instruments: the necessity to appear to be what he is not is imperiously dictated by affection, as is the necessity to be authentic that follows from his devouring need for truth.

However, one must then establish, on the side of art, a complicity between the means of influence (in this case the Catholic means that Gide's Protestant conscience is suspicious of) and his own shameful sensibility; what is the attraction that here plies the power of the Catholic and voluptuous genius of Claudel? Shocked by Gide's admiration for Nietzsche, Claudel wrote to him that "no man is great in himself, but rather by the way in which he harmonizes with his environment and the degree to which this harmony enriches and instructs the rest of mankind."[ix] But it is precisely this accord that is prohibited by Gide's nature, and when Claudel declares that he is saved because he has grasped that art and religion should not be antagonistically posited in us, but that they should also not be confused, Gide will already be too inclined toward conceiving art not as any kind of transposition but rather as a means of producing hidden things.[9]

The more Claudel exerts himself in arguments, images, and exhortations with the reticent Gide, the more he deepens the gap between them; from their first contacts Gide has judged Claudel: "a steam hammer," "a fixed

---

ix. *The Correspondence Between Paul Claudel and André Gide*, letter dated 08/07/03 (38/4).

cyclone," a being in whom the violence of pathos carries and directs the intelligence, while in Gide precisely the opposite is the case, or so he believes. To such an extent that when Claudel claims to distinguish art and evangelism, Gide will grasp nothing less than the magnificent success of an unconscious deception. "The greatest advantage of religious faith, for the artist, is that it permits him a limitless pride."[x] "Religious certainty gives this robust mind a deplorable infatuation."[xi]

Nevertheless, one cannot be content with saying that Gide has a temperament suited to dialogue, and that, although he had secretly taken a "position" as soon as Claudel wanted to begin it, he also asked to be discovered. Nor can one simply note that Claudel has a peremptory nature and possesses a coherence that does not permit another's experience to contradict it. It is just as necessary to recognize that if Gide's inclination for dialogue ultimately splits in two, indeed disassociates itself, this is because there is a fundamental incoherence at the origin of this aptitude. An incoherence between what at first glance seemed to be only desire, partiality [appetence], and the human world organized according to the principle of analogy between natural and human ends, a world where Gidean desire cannot find its object, an incoherence on the order of a much more profound demand that can be satisfied only by obtaining from reason the right to break with the analogical principle of the world. Claudel is in harmony with this principle from which the traditional vision of the world follows, and reason serves this symbiosis. But, if reason is always reason according to one side or another, then one must admit that for Gide this very reason protests against the symbiosis that it has constructed for people other than him. There is hardly any need to emphasize here that according to Claudel this symbiosis almost merges with the *ratio* of the Scholastics that assures the correspondence between Creation, Man, and the Creator; however, according to Gide, this demand does not have its source in the methodical doubt of Cartesian reason, but rather in the spirit's mistrust in the face of its own constructions, of the dependencies that result from them and that would deprive it of the absolute freedom of perpetually recommencing its activity. Perhaps it is correct to expect that Gide would push his aptitude for contraries to the point of putting reason back into question—to the mutual identity of contraries.

But here perhaps the fact that he resides at the heart of both dialectic and dogma is just a characteristic trait of his physiognomy; moreover, this great writer's thought has never assumed an even slightly "professional" shape—it is the thought of someone privileged, who conducts his private life in complete independence, an aristocratic type of thought that has now

x. Ibid. (47/10).
xi. Ibid., journal entry dated 05/16/07 (63/27).

almost vanished. Instead of looking for metaphysical arguments in order to justify himself, Gide has been careful to comment on his life in the language of honest gentlemen, according to classical reason, remaining faithful to the principle of contradiction. It is thus in the name of the same good sense—which suggests to Claudel's reason abdication before faith—that Gide will smell in him the worst sort of despotism that the spirit can suffer. But between the despotism of faith and that no less irrational one of one's own affectivity, quite contrary to putting reason back into question in favor of what he qualifies as "counternature," Gide has chosen and maintained reason as arbiter. Had the irrational affectivity been less pressing, this arbiter would not have had so many chances to intervene: we must attribute its constant intervention in all of the final reflections that Gide has given us exclusively to the intransigent probity of Gide's mind.

Gide initially gave a spiritually unstable impression of himself, perhaps out of fear of wounding his interlocutor by leaving himself open, but if then this timidity becomes guile once he opts to conceal or hide himself, guile becomes habitual for him in his relations with the poet. And if Claudel's blunt advances are followed by retreats sometimes no less blunt, Gide creates the appearance of new hopes and to a certain extent maintains them perhaps more than he wants to, allowing Claudel new opening moves. This is why he generally responds to Claudel only with equivocations, often with pretexts that leave a gap—but a pathetic one—because one feels strongly here the sickness and perhaps also the pain that proves that one spirit cannot show itself to another that it admires and by which it feels itself fully measured, one that it does not want to lose, but that it already knows it will lose as soon as it is discovered. Perhaps this is the cause of the seemingly demonic nuance of Gide's relation to Claudel. It is strange how Claudel's excessive zeal projects an infernal glimmer upon Gide's perplexity. Whether this is a matter of a perplexity before himself or one that results from the necessity of dissimulating, it always follows from the fact that occasionally Gide is led by a certain style of reasoning that, at the end of a proposition, comes back to destroy the original affirmation.

Let us highlight [relevons] the exchange of letters in this correspondence on the subject of *Strait Is the Gate*.[10] After having spoken of the emotion that his reading provoked in him, Claudel twice rushes right to the precipice: the first time, he does not realize that he is merely stating Gide's secret thought: "If the love of God necessarily robbed him (that is, the saint) of the contrition and humility of a penitent heart, *it would almost be better for him to remain in sin*."[11] The second time he gets to the very heart of the question, though it is still veiled under the form of the case of Alissa: "you are taking up again the oldest Quietist blasphemy . . . according to which piety has no need of reward, and that the most noble love is the most disinterested. How could the love of God be perfect, since it would be completely unreasonable, having no cause at all?"[xii] Gide's response is strange: he pleads first for the virtue of the drama made possible by "unorthodoxy" and makes use of a grievance against Catholicism: "I can't imagine what *the* Catholic drama could be. It seems to me that there isn't one; that there cannot and must not be one—or better one could say that it is comprised in the Mass. Catholicism can and must bring peace and certitude, etc., to the soul; *an admirable mechanism is employed here—* it is a *palliative [quiétif]*, not a *motive* for drama. Protestantism, on the contrary, leads the soul along certain fortuitous paths that may end in the way I have described. . . . It is a school of heroism."[12] Up to this point, everything seems to indicate the choice in favor of a spiritual atmosphere where drama is possible, a positive value that Gide vainly seeks in Catholic spirituality. But the phrase that begins with "It is a school of heroism" is continued by a relative clause that immediately ruins the choice for drama: "It is a school of heroism, the error of which, I believe, my book brings out quite well; it lies precisely in that sort of superior infatuation, that heady contempt for any reward (which you took offense at), that gratuitous reversion to the spirit of Corneille. But it can be accompanied by real nobility . . . , etc."[13] What does this mean? Gide claims he wants to live in "unorthodoxy" only because he can express drama in unorthodoxy alone—this drama that is only authentic in unorthodoxy; he distrusts the *admirable mechanism* of Catholicism and refuses to submit to it because in his eyes it risks evading the motive for drama. But he recognizes that this will to remain in drama—the uncaused love of God, in other words the love that has no other object than love, which is nothing other than a piety that is in some way idolatrous—is a superior infatuation. All of this would be fallacious if it didn't hide something else.

In 1912, Claudel asked Gide where the *N.R.F.* stood in regard to the doctrine regarding "the decadence of Art due to its separation from what people so stupidly call Morality, and which I call the Life, the Way and the Truth."[xiii] But, the day before, Gide noted in his *Journal* (not cited by Mallet) that a conversation with Paul-Albert Laurens lead him to glimpse the possibility of writing *Corydon* in an entirely different mode.[14] A few days later, he finds himself in Switzerland at Neuchâtel and he writes in his *Journal* (cited by Mallet): "Have I reached the limit of experience? And will I be able to grasp myself anew? I need to make wise use of my remaining energy. How easy it would be for me now to throw myself into a confessional! How difficult it is to be at one and the same time, for oneself, he who commands and he who obeys! But what spiritual director would understand with sufficient subtlety this vacillation, this passionate indecision of my whole being, this equal aptitude for contraries. A depersonalization so voluntarily and so difficultly

xii. Ibid.
xiii. Ibid., letter dated 01/15/12 (177/128).

obtained, that could be explained and excused only by the production of the works that it authorizes and with an eye to which I have worked to suppress my own preferences." And further on: "But can one still make resolutions when one is over forty? One lives according to twenty-year-old habits." A few resolutions to educate his will by the most everyday means then follow: "Never go out without a definite aim; hold to this." On the evening of the same day he noted that all this quickly seemed absurd to him—that he again became conscious of his strength. "This state is the very one I wanted; but as soon as I weaken, I cease to be anyone because I have wanted to be all (perfect state of the novelist), for fear of being only *someone*."[15] Other mentions of this tendency toward division, toward the depersonalization that seizes him and that, once he has recovered, he is afraid to utilize as a faculty, may be found in his *Journal*. It is a phenomenon (that we must return to) which will be repeated so often that on the decisive day [*grand jour*] he will not produce the grave question that absorbs him. So many convolutions, oscillations, qualifications: what remains *unsaid does not exist*, because he has not yet become the object of a universal judgment that will fall upon him. When Gide has finally made his profession of faith largely public, he will have simultaneously broken with the traditional moral world and definitively consolidated the feeling of his own authority. It is then that, brought onto the very terrain of the adversary, the battle that unfurled within the limits of a particular case will find its universal justification in the destruction of the preeminent site of the social values: the family, "home of all egoisms."

But, on the day after the notes cited above, his malaise acquires the physiognomy of the very person upon whom his claim for not speaking his rancor falls: *I wish I had never known Claudel. His friendship weighs on my thought, and obligates and embarrasses it. I still cannot bring myself to hurt him, but as my thought affirms itself it is opposed to his. How can I explain myself to him? I would willingly leave the whole field to him, I would abandon everything. But I cannot say something different from what I have to say, which cannot be said by anyone else* (cited by Mallet).[xiv] This malaise must have been expressed; we do not know under what form, nor in what terms, in a letter (also disappeared) to Claudel, since the latter judges it enigmatic. And one can scarcely imagine in what state of mind Gide must have received these lines from the poet in response: "Perhaps I will shock you by telling you the foundation of my thought, which is that you have for a long time been, like all men in the labor of conversion, under the influence of the devil who is furious at seeing you escaping from him. Like all extremely sensitive and nervous people, you are perhaps more exposed than others to this sinister influence. I had this idea

---

xiv. *The Correspondence Between Paul Claudel and André Gide*, letter dated 01/??/12 (178/129), translation modified.

like a flash upon reading *Saul* and *The Immoralist*, and it came back to me last night."[xv] Claudel evokes the issue of temptation and the power of resisting it. The invitation is clear, Claudel wants to lead Gide to speak: "you are undone by this idea that by something you could say, do, or write, you could discourage, disconcert, or scandalize me. The most reckless fantasies do not bother me at all: my own heart has often served as a parade ground for them!"[16] He wants Gide to escape from the dialogue with himself and come to find him so "that we can talk for a good while together tranquilly and calmly, for there is nothing that horrifies our Enemy as much as good sense."[17] Gide's response— also among the lost letters—tells Claudel of Valery Larbaud's conversion to Catholicism, which perhaps was an excellent occasion to elude his own case but results in reassuring Claudel not only of Gide's susceptibility, but also of "the rumors that claim that the book that you are preparing will be 'terrible' (?)."[18] Then setting out from what he believes is an established fact, namely that Gide knows and recognizes Christ, he explains to Gide the sacramental conception of the Savior in the Church, the meaning of the *real presence* which postulates that the love of God can also be satisfied by possession, forgetting that what is at the very heart of his conception of the universe would in Gide's mind be again reflected only as the *admirable contrivance* that evades the drama—and finally comes to the mystical Body: "You yourself know that one cannot be part of a body of people and still preserve all of your freedom to act and believe as you want."[19] Because, according to Claudel's postulate, Gide believes in Christ but does not belong to the Church, he is "like a defaulting debtor," and because Gide has still "given nothing," "justice has not been satisfied."[20] Claudel thinks it is his duty to cite as an example for him the return of diverse dissident theologians to an orthodox conception of the Church, and he encourages Gide to present *his objections* to him *formally* [*présenter ses objections en forme*], which would facilitate the discussion.

In order to encourage him in this way, Claudel must not be willing to veer from his idea of Gide at all: a Protestant fallen into passive disbelief thanks to the dogmatic anarchy of his Church but one who can be brought back by rational means; it must also be the case that Gide by his attitude left Claudel to struggle with this phantom of himself, allowing nothing to leak out concerning his Christ negator of the family, Christ against the Churches, nor most important that he had found in Christ the master [*maitre*] of his own unbelief. How could Gide put his "objections formally"? Every one of Gide's objections was precisely lacking all "form."

We come to the crucial moment of this correspondence, when, in the middle of March 1914, Claudel reads with astonishment in the *N.R.F.*, where *The Caves of the Vatican* was first published, a "pederastic passage which," he

---

xv. Ibid., letter dated 02/29/12 (179/131), translation modified.

writes to Rivière, "throws a sinister light upon certain of our friend's previous works."[21] And the same day he writes a violent admonition to Gide. Does Gide not know that after *Saul* and *The Immoralist* there is no further imprudence to commit? Will he answer yes or no as to whether he is himself a participant in these horrible practices? If he is silent or is evasive in his response, Claudel will know what restrains him. If he is not, why this strange predilection for this kind of subject? "And if you are, you unhappy man, cure yourself and do not spread these abominations. Consult Madame Gide; consult the better half of your heart."[22]

Gide's response is certainly the only moving one of this collection, and doubtless one of the most troubling documents that we have of his intimate life. The most revelatory pages of his *Journal*, written without witness, do not bear this copy [*décalque*] of himself beneath the gaze of an other who judges. And if, in his *Journal*, Gide often refutes the judgment brought against him by someone who is absent, it is never like in this letter where, under the searching gaze of a friend, he undergoes a metamorphosis; this metamorphosis is truly, as far as he is concerned, completely unreal—at most he will no longer appear as the one he was in the eyes of someone else, but in the eyes of this latter, he will suddenly assume a monstrous physiognomy and he cannot but terrify him. What Gide experiences here as a summation is the brute necessity of appearing in his true light and of finally showing his face, a unique face that, as Claudel surmises, will allow him to identify Gide once and for all, while this face will necessarily still be one that is, to his detriment, composed for him.

In his response, Gide more than anything shows himself to be preoccupied with preserving and handling carefully his wife's affection. This is the essential reason for his mental reservations toward opinion in general and particularly toward Claudel. Indirectly, he makes Claudel understand this. Then comes the confession: I have never experienced desire before a woman—a confession, given under its negative form, that consequently implies the positive confession that Gide still refuses to formulate explicitly. But Gide, if he is trying to lessen the shock that this negative confession will produce, aggravates it by taking a repentant attitude: he makes recourse to the sacramental secret of confession and by that enters anew into the game with Claudel. A protestation of honor and candor follows, but this protestation is still tinged with ambiguity: on the one hand, he pleads in favor of literary frankness [*parrhesie litteraire*] and against social and moral untruthfulness; on the other hand, he begs Claudel not to see in this phrase an appreciation for other morals, or even other desires. Then he stops himself, and this in the very name of the Christian idea of vocation: "By what cowardice, since God calls me to speak, should I have evaded this question in my books? *I have not chosen to be this way.*"[23] Since Gide has come forth in this way from the hands of the Creator, God has chosen him to bear before the consciousness of men the enigma that he represents. It is a sounding of Claudel's Catholic spirit.

But Gide, who is anguished by the possible consequences of this first confession, and also worried that some snare may have been set for him, without waiting for Claudel's reaction, reaffirms to him the next day that he has confided in him as in a priest, and that God is certainly using Claudel in order to speak to him, a reaffirmation meant to put the friendship with Claudel to the test and to limit the consequences that his zeal might bring. Now Gide claims that perhaps it would be preferable for Claudel to betray him; by his reckoning he would thereby be freed from everything that Claudel represents in his eyes—which so often arrests and hinders him. Gide here wants to hasten the decision: Claudel finally snaps, and Gide continues on his way without this awkward companion. And nevertheless a chance remains: everything could be changed in an instant. One has the impression that Gide is waiting for the decisive turn of his own destiny to come from Claudel, for he concludes thus: *In truth I do not see how to resolve this problem that God has inscribed in my flesh*.[24] This phrase ought to ring in Claudel's soul as a cry of distress and consequently encourage him to respond to him as he did, because Gide claims his abnormal constitution is attributable to God. But either Gide still believes in a transcendent paradox, in an election that he consents to judge from the point of view of theology; or, already unbelieving, this is no longer a problem to resolve but is best liquidated within his own consciousness, since he already wrote *Corydon*; and having written this book, he has surpassed the pathetic phase of the problem, as he put it to Marcel Drouin in 1911—a book written not at all in order to move to pity, but in order to discomfort [*gêner*].[25] And as he cannot bring himself to discomfort Claudel, he moves him to pity.

For Claudel, these two letters (both sent from Florence) constitute an unhoped-for occasion—so unhoped for that he immediately jeopardizes the human means for a conversion of Gide to Catholicism. (Gide himself said that his letter [of confession] and Claudel's response were an event in his life. Later, many years later—it is impossible to know to what extent this was meant to express some regrets—Gide will make an allusion to some circumstances when conversion seemed immanent to him, and he will almost say that the Catholic faith opened up [*épanoui*] his own qualities. Can one push the coquetry further?)

Claudel is just as exposed as Gide. He begins by stating that he does not know what would give him the right to judge someone, even though he judges the tendency and that, the tendency not being separable from the subject, he cannot avoid condemning the subject. Claudel immediately attacks homosexual morals and a possible system of defense that he perceives in Gide. If sexual attraction does not have as an outcome its natural end which is reproduction, it is deviant and wicked. Claudel then refers to the condemnation of this vice by Revelation and Scripture, in particular by Saint Paul. But Gide doesn't need Claudel to know this. And if Gide poses the question of a homosexual *nature*, independently of all habit, now Claudel does not permit Gide to be judged a victim of a Protestant heredity that habituated him to seek the rules for his actions only in himself. Thus he insists essentially on the *acts* and claims that the fear of God is sufficient for a man to resist his abnormal instincts. If Gide tells him of his horror of hypocrisy, Claudel retorts that cynicism is worse. Gide must become aware of the grave responsibility that he is taking on, given the prestige conferred by his intelligence, by making himself the apologist for a vice that is spreading more and more. Finally, shifting to an explicitly pragmatic plane, Claudel puts him on guard against universal reprobation, and he points to a flagrant contradiction in Gide's attitude: "I will keep an absolute silence, but it is you who talk and make a show of yourself." He adds this assurance, which leaves one wondering: "And have no doubt of this: that on the day that everyone has abandoned you, you will still have me. I know the incomparable worth of a soul."[26]

A *postscriptum* follows in order to dissipate Gide's fears: "What an absurd idea!" He assures him that he has only written of this matter to three trustworthy persons, to Jammes (*"a simple exclamation"*); to Rivière[27] whose soul he has taken under his tutelage; and finally to the abbot Fontaine, under the seal of confession. "No one dares to say anything to you. I'm the only one who dares to speak bluntly to you and I'm brave enough because of the interest that I take in your soul . . . and don't think that I am in any way responsible if the scandal that you have unleashed bursts." As a guarantee of discretion, he returns the two letters to Gide and concludes: "For my part, your two beautiful and noble letters heighten my sense of relief. You have confessed to me."[28] Nevertheless, in the same letter, Claudel has asked Gide to make two gestures: first to suppress the "pederastic" passage of *The Caves* when it is published as a book; then to go see a priest, the abbot Fontaine, whom Claudel seems to have written to only in order to prepare him for this consultation.

In reading Gide's response, he seems stronger, and with good reason. He parries, since it is inevitable that he will appear as defensive, and is audacious enough to protest: "where can you see in my two letters anything that resembles an apology or even an excuse? I am simply telling you *how things stand*." He asks him for the address of the abbot F but robs Claudel in advance of any hope that the latter puts in this consultation: "if the most fervent and faithful love has not been able to obtain any acquiescence from my flesh, I leave it to you to imagine the effect of his exhortations, reprimands, and counsels. (And, I ask you, what *meaning* does your phrase have for me: "In spite of all the doctors, I obstinately refuse to believe in a physiological determinism"?)" Gide cannot agree to the suppression of the incriminating passage. "No, do not ask me either to doctor or to compromise; or it will be I who think less of you." And taking a reprimanding tone in turn, he vehemently reproaches

Claudel for having told [*alerté*] Rivière for whom Gide has the strongest reverence. "You have given in to a thoughtless fit of anger." The absurdities, the monstrosities that Rivière will imagine will force Gide to burden him with confidences that he had wanted to spare him. "Goodbye. Believe that my friendship for you has never been stronger."[29] Thus the most frank letter that Gide wrote to Claudel—at least in this collection (we are leaving aside what might be contained in those that were lost in "the Tokyo earthquake")—is also concluded by one of the most sincere statements. Whenever he is on the verge of being separated from someone to whom he finds himself in some way attached, Gide, apart from any dependence, can truly love them for their own sake and experience their value freely.

If, at this time, Gide had still been able to be shaken, nothing could have done it more poorly than Claudel's way of intervening in his tribulations, insofar as they were then real. For Claudel sodomy is not thinkable except as a vice developed by habit, a deliberately exercised perversion. Claudel's conception, based on the Scholastic notion of *habitus* and independent of all moral discrimination, would perhaps be closer to the modern psychiatric concepts than to any paltry scientism of Gide's. It is a completely different question in that register. Homosexuality is a natural phase that is more or less pronounced in an individual's sexual development and which is organized into a psychic complex only when the individual is stuck in this phase.

But Claudel does not hesitate to put sodomy on the same plane as onanism or phenomena as different from each other as vampirism, pedophilia, and cannibalism, and he postulates that the justification of the first would entail the justification of all the rest (which he had, on the contrary, perfect reason to claim if, instead of Gide, he was speaking of a certain libertine philosopher of the eighteenth century, who was capable of rationalizing any such disposition).[30] It was a question here of knowing to what extent Gide, interpreting his own case according to physiological determinism, did not offer Claudel a means of breaking the dilemma that Gide imagined: God *or homosexuality*. But Claudel brusquely rejected as blasphemous the lone idea of an irreducible, normal constitution that, at least subjectively, constituted the ground of Gide's experience, regardless of what produced Gide's interpretive error in this matter; according to him this idea can only express the distress of a man who is the "victim of his Protestant heredity." Saying this a long time before pinning Gide in the pillory, he forces him from now on, as though he still even needed to force him, to lean on the "pillory" and thus to give his own face to this "vice." In a word, instead of freeing him he definitively imprisons him in his dilemma, by having worsened the terms: God *or* Sodom—which amounts to assigning Gide to a forced residence in the homosexual ghetto.

At the same time, by going before the priest, Claudel also ruined the image of the confessor in Gide's thought. Moreover the auricular confession is here found to be in agreement not with the need for a public confession, but rather with the need for a profession of faith. Nothing, in effect, could be as repugnant to Gide as seeing his tendencies—involuntarily clandestine—"benefiting" the confessional, when on the contrary he is waiting for the hour to proclaim them. To secretly avow as faults to the tribunal of the Church desires or acts he experienced or consented to as a natural necessity, and whose reiteration—wrongly or rightly—appears to him inescapable, in his eyes this was cheating in order to be redeemed. From the point of view of his discussion with Claudel that began so poorly, for Gide to enter into a confessional amounts to being thrown into sacrilege. But if there is something that Gide is horrified by, it is being portrayed in the light of Satanism that constitutes the literary prestige of some authors. Revolting against Montfort's interpretation ("M. Gide wants to be a sinner, he desires laws in order to taste the pleasure of transgressing them," etc.),[31] he writes in his Journal: "This conception of sin as a sorbet, of sacrilege and Satanism (which was Barbey d'Aurevilly's, for example . . .) is not Protestant at all. Nor is it any more mine for that reason."[32] Shall we claim that if a pederast is already a Protestant it is better for him to remain so than to enter into the Church? We are far from such an absurdity. But here is a bit of the response that Gide himself gave in response to the problem so poorly posed first by Claudel and then by the latter's other Catholic friends: "Better not to enter into it, this is still *the best way of getting out of it*."[xvi] If, however, sensibility is acting here as a deforming mirror and reflects the confessional as a black market—insofar as the "Protestants" are always slightly inclined toward seeing clandestine machinations in the Catholic rites—"stop fooling around or it will end in tears"—this is because in Gide's particular case, Claudel's reaction has reinforced this penchant for suspicion; from now on Gide will "be purified" by his license and will justify homosexuality by making it *public*, while he will suspect the Church, on the other hand, of being an *impure* enterprise.

Moreover, if it is only a matter of heredity, rather than the elaboration of affective reflexes by ancestral habits, Claudel sees in Gide's Protestant heredity only a few habits of thought. He has not discovered the vestiges of the Calvinist feeling of the fallen and condemned nature, a feeling that does not await sanctification by God (as in the Catholic faith), but pardon. For to understand Gide, one must understand that this feeling of a condemned nature is no longer verified as a theological concept, but rather as the personal feeling of his irreducible constitution—thus as the problem that God inscribes in his flesh. From this also arises, for Gide, the tendency toward

---

xvi. Gide is not speaking about himself, but on the subject of the thought of Miguel de Unamuno, whom Claudel charged with heresy. (*Journal*, February 1916) [the entry is actually dated March 14, 1916 (p. 136)—trans.].

splitting, the interest that he takes in the problem of the double, which has also especially haunted Protestant literature: Am I chosen? Am I damned? But chosen, I nonetheless remain a *pardoned* damned, because God, who consents to not seeing my sin in order to admit me, remains *exterior to me*. Whatever my works are, they are agreeable to God only if I consider them as works of sin. I can thus hope to be Godly only if first I recognize being Devilish. From this religion, Gide has retained only the need to retract and disavow an "aptitude" for the other, under the form of splitting, because in the fundamental impossibility of changing the *other* will assume this impossibility that consciousness, relieved, but also a spectator, will be content to describe under the pretext of doing psychology. Such is the meaning of the pseudoconversations of Gide with the Devil, his recent attraction to James Hogg's *Confessions of a Justified Sinner*,[33] and what gives him one more occasion to interpret the Devil as a simple "exteriorization of our own desires," by which he enjoys putting words in his mouth: *Why do you fear me? You know quite well that I don't exist.* Ultimately this is what challenged Gide with the most force, indeed compensated for the need or the absence of need for the auricular confession, insofar as the question could even be really posed.

One can therefore distinguish two periods in the arc of Gide's life: the first, placed entirely under the sign of the secret, which determines the *aptitude for contraries*, and disposes him to splitting, and which runs up to the eve of the publication of *If the Seed Should Die*; *Corydon* and *The Counterfeiters* appear almost simultaneously with this work, and then the period of license begins: it is marked by the disclosure of personal writings in the successive publications of his *Journal*, the most recent of which evince the most virulent confessions. Therefore Gide has lived in order *to ruin*, with his concerns, the traditional notion of *personal life*. By publishing, while living, what other writers of his stature have reserved for posterity, if not for destruction, he has wanted to show that nothing of ourselves justifies the secret (as long as one is careful not to damage the lives of others) and that every personal experience is only ever lived as a function of everyone. With this he extends his battle against familial compartmentalization into the domain of personal life; the secret is equivalent to a psychological and spiritual capitalism, its disclosure to a fungibility of the life of souls. It is a matter of returning to the individual everything that he owes to the human community that always surpasses him, and that he was able to surpass for a moment only in favor of a conjunction of different currents in his own consciousness—a consciousness which must be acquired, along with his experiences, through the existence of everyone.

Having said this, does it mean that everything disclosable truly constitutes the authentic personal life? Is there not something irreducible remaining beyond all imaginable disclosure that we know nothing of and that, precisely by having required this disclosure, would nonetheless remain the *most* authentic—this life that, freed from everything that must be said, would also remain the most intangible, the only privacy that is truly important, the only valuable one.

One day, Gide was happy to offer a sort of commentary on the defects of an old German film, *Nosferatu the Vampire*: "If I were to rewrite the film, I would portray Nosferatu—who we know is the vampire from the beginning—not as a member of a terrible and fantastic species, but on the contrary as having the characteristics of an inoffensive young man, charming and full of kindnesses. First, I would want the dread to arise only through some very weak indications, and in the mind of the spectator before that of the hero. Wouldn't it be much more frightening if he were presented to the woman from the very beginning in such a charming aspect? It is a kiss that must be transformed into a bite. If he shows his teeth immediately, it becomes nothing but a childish nightmare."[34] Let us here give in to the temptation to seek in this fortuitous, excellent digression a sort of reflection of Gide's own image, or at least his own demon, in the mind of right-thinking people. It is in spite of them that Gide has become a sort of spiritual vampire for them. But has he not contributed to no small extent in elaborating this image? Is he not involved in the game? Does he not also make a feint in order to reassure the spectator: *But no, there is nothing terrible, nothing but the quite natural: at most a little too charming*—as he might be imagined doing in this scenario. Does he not also determine that to show his teeth first would be to establish in their minds a definitely nonchildish nightmare that would compromise his true thought? But later he modifies slightly the scenario that he designs here: "I would want him (the vampire) to willingly appear to everyone as a hideous monster; charming only in the eyes of the young woman, a voluntary and seduced victim; but, seduced in his turn, he should be made less and less horrible to the point of *becoming* the delightful being whose mere appearance he at first only borrowed. And it is this delightful being that the cock's crow must kill, that the spectator must see suddenly disappear with relief and regret."[35] Gide instinctively gives here a parable of his own adventure: he is himself simultaneously the young woman, a voluntary and seduced victim (this is his own imagination), and the "monster hideous to all"—this is what he is afraid to appear as, charming only to the eyes of the youth, "a voluntary and seduced victim" as his contemporaries would say; for if the young woman forms here a bit of his own curiosity about the youth, this curiosity itself draws from Gide's youth in order to compose this exquisite being whose mere appearance he first assumed. And if the cock's cry is lethal even when this physiognomy is authentic, this is because it signals the lucidity that puts an end to this game of splitting, of exchange and of influences—for one does not exercise influence with impunity—and which finally announces the man resigned to himself—but, for all that, certainly not satisfied.

Chapter Four

Preface to *A Married Priest*
by Barbey d'Aurevilly

If not the least known of the works by the author of the *Diaboliques* [*The She-Devils*], *A Married Priest* is today certainly the most forgotten. During his lifetime it was also the least appreciated of his books.

Owing precisely to this distance, it appears as an important book that—for better or worse—provides an account of the facticity and authenticity that indissolubly formed the personality of Barbey d'Aurevilly.

If Barbey d'Aurevilly made up a character [*personnage*] of himself destined for the external world, he has also, with this double, presented several portraits that are only relatively self-portraits: such as *Rollon Langrune*, the story's narrator who appears in the Prologue.

Between the author and the "portrait of the author" a crystallization of diverse impulses that must be subordinated to each other is effected in order to obtain a physiognomy and the ambiance that the tableau requires.

What impulses are at work here? Barbey lends certain of his humors and qualities to his double, a bit of his dazzling verve, of his daintiness with a touch of lascivious slyness; and in all of this there is a deep sense of the nobility of melancholy, a predilection for that generosity of the heart that is accepting even to the point of shame and ignominy.

His strongest impulses—aggressiveness and voluptuousness—first appear under the mask of the Catholic polemicist, then under that of the sophisticate. But a violence, a cruelty, a sensual delight in horror such as what explodes several years later in *Les Diaboliques*, are seeking here, in Rollon Langrune's language, to be appeased in a way other than by the evocation of excessive [*effrénés*] scenes and gestures. The appeal of the sea, of forests, the falling light of ancestral places, the spectral return of bygone ages bring, more than a satiety, a more certain deliverance in a pure atmosphere of the flesh's sanies and tears [*déchirements*].

In Rollon Langrune's remarks the fervor of the defender of orthodoxy alternates with the nostalgia for a world of customs that has disappeared beneath social upheavals. The loss of social privileges has nevertheless found a more subtle sort of compensation: the privilege of *exclusive experiences* which henceforth will be affirmed as an authority.

In the world of a society commercialized by notions of *progress* and *utility*—a world that was the torturing context of Baudelaire, Nerval, and of Barbey—exclusive experiences, in the same way as poetic creation, are marked with the stigma of the *useless*. For Baudelaire, for Nerval—in other ways for Nietzsche—the useless character of exclusive experiences resides in this statement of Thomas de Quincey: the *Burden of the incommunicable*.[1] Between the *incommunicable* and the hostile social world there are attitudes of declared or larval refusal, or even provisional compromise. Dandyism, more important for Barbey than for Baudelaire, is borne as the mask of this authority and privilege that conferred the exclusive experiences, and also as the appropriate mask to hide the stigma of the *useless*.

On the social plane, dandyism, in order to escape from its own vulgarization, has recourse to paradox; it is this aspect of dandyism that Barbey introduced into the genre of polemical writing, in the name of the legitimist and Catholic reaction against the bourgeois, positivist, and secularizing spirit. Here, his aggressiveness developed all of its verve. "Lamartine claims that I am a *villain* all the more *atrocious* because I am great (*sic*), that *I am a Catholic Marat* (is this why I am great? . . .) *and that I paint the guillotine white* (*sic*)."[2] Barbey reports this statement by Lamartine with an indignant satisfaction. To appear as a *villain* all the more *atrocious* because one *is great*, Barbey willingly submits to the *nihil obstat*.[3] Here, in effect, owing to a *stubborn fin de non-reçevoir*[4] in opposition to social convulsions despite a perfectly lucid vision of the event, there is a great danger that the paradox will turn into deliberate "bad faith" in the eyes of the faithless. Dandyism is combined in a bizarre way with an intellectual *Chouannerie* that others, with a status much inferior to his own, will exploit with less genius and more dishonesty.[5] According to the axiom that there is no truth for the enemies of truth—no morality is spared in the eyes of those contemptuous of the dogma that alone grounds morality—every mystification is permitted both in their own eyes as well as in the eyes of a world that has lost the sense of mystery and from now on only wants to depend on man.

However, under the pretext of defending orthodoxy and monarchy, Barbey is nevertheless not actually taking up again the position of a Joseph de Maistre.[6] What he *knows how to* defend intimately, what properly belongs to him, is the *incommunicable* of his exclusive experiences, and this is why the Aurevillian paradox, especially in poetic creation, steeps its reasons in a negative theology and is explained in the figures of that theology.

Thus aggressive violence is insufficient for the polemic, which wastes it instead; this is only an exterior and social manner of refuting, by means of paradox, human respect with its adherents and successes; nevertheless it seeks on the contrary a terrain where it can confess beneath a suggestive and communicable form—but disguised and always compatible with an equivocal interpretation—its complicity with the nameless forces that are only "shadows" in the eyes of "human respect."

The novelistic fabrication that here fully realizes this function has the advantage of enriching the exegetical range of everything that it imagines without losing any of the combative efficacy of this paradox: against the century's humanitarianism, this infamy that must be crushed in its turn, developing inhuman pleasure in the name of a hidden God. *A Married Priest* is more illustrative of this than *Les Diaboliques* [*De qu'illustre Un prêtre marié autant que Les Diaboliques*].

It is a dangerous game. For it provides weapons against religion and, what's more, it abounds with a sense of voluntarism—in order to vindicate again all the old [*retenus*] grievances against religion as so many positive values, which are decried as immoral and injurious by humanitarians of all tendencies. But Sade, by his own confession, in an opposed but analogous sense, previously thought that he had furnished the "devout soil" [*"tourbe devotieuse"*] with all the weapons needed against atheism in order to push it to its extreme consequences: to the knowledge of an absolute amoralism.[i]

---

i. Cf. Marquis de Sade, *Cahiers personnels (1803–1804)*, unedited texts, collected, prefaced, and annotated by Gilbert Lély (Paris, Corrêa, 1953).

We can never thank Gilbert Lély enough for having restored to us, among other texts, the quite singular *Note Regarding My Detention*, which dates from Sade's internment at Bicêtre in 1803. Commenting on this note, in which the author of *Justine*, after always being defended for having written it, still supports his disavowal, "since it is as the author of such a work that he was sequestered at Bicêtre," M. Gilbert Lély observes that "at the beginning of the nineteenth century when the revenge of the priests is announced, the marquis vituperates against himself for having inadvertently served the cause of the defenders of God by writing for the public the novel *Justine* in which all the corrupt heroes are atheist philosophers."

In the *Note Regarding My Detention* Sade argues in his defense as follows:

"When one reads it (the novel *Justine*) attentively, then one will see that, by an unforgivable blunder, by a deliberate (as he understands it) procedure to blend the author with the sages and fools, with the good and the wicked, all the philosophical personages of this novel (that is to say *the atheists*) "are gangrenous and villainous. However I am a philosopher; all those who know me do not doubt that it is my pride and my profession. . . . And can one admit for a moment, even supposing me to be a fool, can one, I say, suppose for a minute that I would pollute with horrors and execrations the character with which I most honor myself? . . . Do you see such horrors in my other works?" [Sade is making an allusion to *Aline and Valcour*.] "On the contrary, all the villains that I have painted are of the faithful, because all of the faithful are wicked and all philosophers are honest men. . . . Therefore

In an age where socially and practically acquired atheism is beginning to construct its morality in the name of the freedom of conscience, Barbey d'Aurevilly thinks only of ruining this morality in the name of dogma by pushing religious strictness to the absolute of the passions. Morally, Sade the atheist and Barbey the Catholic are nihilists.

What exactly has happened? Nothing less than the divorce of religion and morality followed immediately, on the one hand, by that of bourgeois morality and (scientific) reason and, on the other, by that of reason and mystery. On the eve of this total disintegration of the mental structures of society, what exactly is the position of a Catholic polemicist such as Barbey?

It is likely that the author of A Married Priest and of the Diaboliques has, if not actually thought, at least perfectly *sensed* that the laicizing principles, in particular the freedom of conscience, were of a directly Christian inspiration, and that through these principles he could attack nothing less than Christian morality pure and simple. Even if this means that he no longer retains Catholic orthodoxy and, as an apologist, only further exalts structures that are the most foreign to the evangelic spirit—but also the most Caesarian, the most "Machiavellian," the most inquisitorial; for to him it is a majestic edifice, well-fashioned from prohibitions and ambiguous signs revolving around the Host as a symbol of a Passionate magic, where the Precious Blood and Sin, the celestial and the wicked flesh, are simultaneously polarized. Here, in effect, not only hatred for the laicizing, mercantile, and disbelieving century, nostalgia for a spiritual hierarchy that is responsive to the privilege of exclusive experiences, often drawing the allure from a defense of its menaced institutions, but equally and above all a most secret aspiration is able to find here its appeasement in the practice of an intimate magic. For in magic, that mirror of the ambiguity of the passions, some of the forces that are most obscure but also most apt to masquerade are aggressiveness and voluptuousness, along with their corollary: morose delectation, each struggling and colluding in turn with their own fatality.

It is within such an *edifice* that Barbey d'Aurevilly is found installed, entrenched, when he sets out to write simultaneously A Married Priest and Les

---

it is not true that *Justine* is by me. Even more I say: it is impossible for it to be . . . I would here add something even stronger: that it is very singular that all of the devoted dirt, Geoffroy, Genlis, Legouvé, Chateaubriand, La Harpe, Luce de Lancival, Villeterques, that all of these brave agents of the tonsure would rage against *Justine*, since this book has actually aided their cause. Had they tried, they could not have paid for such a well-made work as this one in order to denigrate philosophy. And I swear on everything sacred that I have in the world that I will never forgive myself for having served these individuals who are so incredibly mistaken about me." (*Cahiers personnels*, pp. 63–65.)

Barbey d'Aurevilly goes on, in his own novels, to work out this *deliberate procedure to blend the author with the sages and fools.*

Diaboliques, some of which are prior, others later than *A Married Priest*. *Les Diaboliques* illustrate the tension between celestial and wicked flesh. *A Married Priest* offers an account of the same divorce between religion and morality, between reason and mystery, with all of the consequences that follow in the destiny of the man who "takes the side" of mystery, and who, despite having reason for an option, remains dependent on mystery. Recounted in the language of orthodoxy, the staging of this destiny provides an account of a magic valorization of both prohibitions and signs, in this case those of the sacramental order that links the priest to the Host.

On March 14, 1855, Barbey d'Aurevilly writes to Trébutien: "I am myself *ensorcelled* [*encaprice*] by a strange subject and my verve has suffered powerfully! as it always suffers the hussy! when it awakens naturally in me. This strange subject that will bear the very dignified title of its strangeness: *le Chateau des soufflets* [*The Castle of the Bellows*] is a novel of a certain daring and freshness—not long! A dozen or so serials (a volume)—but *hooking* [*crochetant*] the attention and interest, just as thieves, armed with claws, hook a door and throw it down. You will see, my friend, you will see, but only when it is finished. As for that other one, I have not crystallized. I am possessed by the same subject. I sing in my register and in my chords."[7] In the autumn of the same year, he sends the (first) manuscript to Trébutien: "I am quite sure that you will read it as one must . . . *reading and not running through*, and enduring the deliberate and carefully thought-out gradations of the author's perambulations and curtain-raising. . . . The first thing that I will do after the *Soufflets* and *Des Touches*[8] will be something vast and full of intrigue. But like a sensitive and caring group, in some corner of the countryside, this *castle of bellows, which I want you to be interested in as in a person*, is not to be rudely rejected. There is in it the tone of a brusque story, hardy, familiar, which is not the tone of everything, and for the poets, for whom a motif plays before a poem, there is also a basis for a beautiful dream. Will you like it Calixte, will you? Sultan of asceticism, will you throw the handkerchief to this Christian martyr who, I hope, is more true, more human and less theatrical than Cymodocée,[9] and who dies from the bites of her father—a terrible lion in his own right! You will see!"[ii]

After many revisions over an interval of almost ten years, the novel will appear in serials in *Pays* in 1864, under its definitive title: *A Married Priest*, before being published in a volume by A. Faure in 1865. The mere change of the original title itself reveals the displacement of the interest that the author uses to treat the chosen theme. The first title, more "picturesque" and mysterious, makes allusion to the topographical aspect of the story and at the same time to the particular activity of the hero: the *bellows* of a laboratory.

---

ii. *Lettres à Trébutien*, v. 3, pp. 338–339, letter dated September 21–22, 1855.

The preference given to the second title, which indicates the situation of the hero, a title with a polemical and apologetic bearing, is directed at the same time toward the audience of Catholics and to lay opinion. It is a matter of striking at the latter for its reprobation of the celibacy of priests. The book's lack of success, if one excepts the interest that it aroused in the author's native province, the negative reactions from both sides indicate an unease and a misunderstanding provoked first of all by the title. For *married* means *atheist*.

No one, at that time, perhaps not even Trébutien, seems to have been able to read "enduring the deliberate and carefully thought-out gradations of the author's perambulations and the curtain-raising." The curtain neither reveals nor merely hides the action, but its perambulation and its raising themselves allow for a reading of the inverse side of the tapestry. The weft here is crossed by that thread that forms the apologist and his argument: a married priest. But the threads that cross it and converge on the intelligibility of the figures form an ensemble of motifs on the reverse that are the ones that we retain and that still affect us today. And we in the future understand better, we understand in a different way than his contemporaries, what Trébutien could not understand in the commentary that Barbey addressed to him: "a novel of a certain daring and newness—but *hooking* [*crochetant*] the attention and the interest, just as thieves, armed with claws, hook a door and throw it down."

The drama of the abbot Sombreval[iii] unfolds through the persistence of the SACRED in the soul of an unbelieving priest. By virtue of the "objective"

---

iii. Here is the real adventure that provides Barbey with the elements of his intrigue: it follows almost word for word the story of a certain abbot, Jean Lebon of Saint-Saveur-le-Vicomte, an ordained priest during the Revolution, charged with a secret mission by his émigré bishop to Jersey, who returned to Paris in order to negotiate the conditions for the return of the prelate with the government, but, in the interval, studied with the chemist Fourcroy, became his disciple, adopted some scientific ideas, was defrocked, and then married the daughter of his teacher. Mme. Lebon, held in ignorance of her husband's priestly past, learned of it while she was pregnant by him and died in childbirth, giving premature birth to a partially paralyzed boy. The widowed father raised this child: and, despite his infirmity, he became a beautiful adolescent who showed a remarkable intellectual precocity, then died at the age of eighteen. (Cf. Jean Canu, *Barbey d'Aurevilly*, Paris, Laffont, 1945.) Such are the initial facts that inspired Barbey for his novel. But it carries an important modification: he has made a young girl, the beautiful and chaste Calixte who is suffering from a mysterious illness, out of the son of the defrocked abbot. As for the defrocked abbot himself, he gives him a Titanesque physiognomy, and he places the two characters in an ambiance that plainly has no relation to the real circumstances. M. Jean Canu tells us directly that when the ex-abbot Lebon returned to his country, which was also Barbey's, and to the environs of Saint-Saveur-le-Vicomte, he acquired the chateau of Quesnay—just as Sombreval does in the novel—and then lived there in perfect security without being

operation of the sacrament, one is ordained a priest by receiving the indelible seal: even if he should abandon himself to debauchery, brigandage, or murder, the mass that he says will always be valid. Neither debauched, nor initially a criminal, but having lost his faith, Sombreval determines that the sacrament he received, emptied, however, of all content by his own judgment and reduced to a pure playacting, no longer has any effect on his actions. Thus he marries, and then becomes a widower and the father of a sick girl, who thinks of nothing but devoting all the resources of science to fight the illness. Lay opinion asks: "This man has a clear conscience, why are you trying to pick a fight with him? And how can one attribute the horrible misfortunes that overwhelm this widower, a devoted father to his daughter, to divine anger?"

But, his case is infinitely more serious than if he had given himself over to debauchery. And Barbey, staging the character and his refusal in order to perpetuate a sinister comedy, wisely sees here the prejudice of the reader, who, spontaneously, applauds only the probity of the hero's conscience.

The abbot Sombreval is married only because he has ceased to believe: for him, as long as it is a matter of a banal demand that priests be allowed to marry, the rupture of sacerdotal celibacy has the value of a protestation of atheism. "If he has left in accordance with the counsel of his atheist conscience," responds the Church, "then he has in fact not left according to the sacerdotal character with which his soul is imprinted forever," and it is by this that dogma, throughout Barbey's book, prevents the lay objection. In the eyes of the Church, it is impossible to see how an atheist could conceive or feel the *material* and *formal* sacrilege if he did not himself have precisely the same

---

otherwise bothered by the populace. Sombreval, on the contrary, installed in this residence, lives there with his daughter as a pariah, and remains there only by defying, with all the force of his contempt, the unbridled hostility of a superstitious population that resents his return as a curse upon the country and his installation at Quesnay as a provocation. It is not at all surprising that in his fictionalization, Barbey wanted his *Married Priest* to have a daughter because of the novelistic advantage to be exploited from the feminine character of Calixte (the expiatory virgin) who is destined to inspire a violent passion in the young Néel of Néhou. This latter character (who incarnates some youthful memories decisive for Barbey) is always presented in the novel as Calixte's double (the "inflation of the vein" on the brow of the young man, in moments of anger, is a copy of the cross-shaped birthmark on the brow of the young girl) and seems like a vestige in Barbey's mind of the son of the abbot Lebon, dead at the age of eighteen. One sees quite clearly the whole course [*fort bien tout le parti*] that a Dostoevsky would draw from the relationship between an atheist father and his believing son. Just so [*tel quel*], the character of Néel remains, nonetheless, latent, the son that Sombreval could have; and the paternal sentiments that Sombreval proves to have for the young man who will never be his son-in-law despite their common desire, as well as the influence that the atheist priest exercises over Néel, are not among the least themes of this novel.

representation that the Church has of it, but positively [*en a positivement*]. This representation that, in order to have been a man of the Church, he shared not long ago, he nevertheless carries within himself as a negative representation, as the judgment that the Church forms of [*porte sur*] him: a sacrilegious priest. Ultimately, he remains so deeply marked in his being by this indelible seal of the sacerdotal which he thought he had effaced from his conscience only because the sign of election is, from now on, one of infamy to him, and it almost propels him into his home country, seeking public outcry as a confrontation in which he will convince himself that he has ceased to be an untouchable, set apart, "sacred," man. However, it is precisely then that he becomes so.

But is Barbey painting a morally tormented soul for us in the character of Sombreval? Not in the slightest. We do not have an affair for a hero of, for example, Bernanos[10] or Graham Greene, authors who have elaborated their torn and contradictory characters under the generalized influence of Dostoevsky's psychology. These latter authors describe spiritual dramas from the interior of a character. Thus their public's receptivity is equally under that same influence, and so very different from the public that Barbey is aiming at.

Not that Barbey does not possess at bottom the subconscious of a *renegade priest*; notwithstanding his romanticism, he proceeds in the manner of an eminently classical artist, still entirely rational in terms of staging, and he portrays a character whose "interior" life he deliberately hides from us—this is why Sombreval is a character composed entirely of one piece, and a steadfast atheist almost to the end. Accordingly, how can the theme of *A Married Priest* be anything less than the repercussion, within a soul, of a gesture that it has had the temerity to commit? within the soul of a priest who has had the audacity to efface the seal, indelible according to the Church, that made of him a man "set apart" forever? But this only reverses the question: How does it happen that Sombreval remains steadfast in his negation of God until the end? Where does he draw this energy from?: according to Barbey, from the indelible seal itself, and from the *divine power that is no less active in its enemies*, as Barbey shows us throughout the book. The gesture of effacing the sacred sign thus becomes indelible; the *erasure* that bars the sign is indelible, indexed to the very indelibility of the sacramental seal. Whence the imperious necessity to repeat the least natural act as a *bar* traced over the *supernatural* world, of repeating the outrage to infinity, because being reorganized according to a subversion that is willed as "absolute," he must pursue this subversion according to the measure of the primitive submission that is also willed and conceived as absolute. *Tu es sacerdos in aeternum* [you are eternally holy]. . . . And this is precisely what constitutes the interest of one aspect of this singular book: the structure of the human soul is made such that it would not know how to act without prohibition, nor could it be constituted without it: in order to sustain itself, the adherence to atheism resus-

citates all the prohibitions that belief is based on—from then on it must fortify itself against its return.

Steadfast in his atheism, Sombreval not only betrays no hint of being a
tormented soul, but seems to be endowed with all of the forces of nature,
henceforth the only reality that he admits. He is an excessive well of learn-
ing, with an unfailing health and a Herculean build: the sovereign man,
promethean, called to make himself master of all the secrets of matter, knowing no duty other than that of procuring worldly benefit for others, the only
thing to which man can aspire. This son of the countryside, denigrator of religion, thus has nothing in common with a Zarathustra other than his scientific fervor that evokes Faust and his sacerdotal past that gives the character
a hint of Mephistophelism, but a quite down-to-earth Mephistophilism.
Moreover, the father of a girl, he displays a paternal passion whose intensity
is equaled only by the violence of his hatred for the superstition that sur-
rounds him, and his sense of justice in the face of the misfortunes of fate. In
sum, behold the sovereign man, ideal of the "positivist" century, that it is now
a matter of striking down: his entire physiognomy is supposed to express only
the revolt against God of an entire presumptuous generation, and his power,
morality, and equity are only the façade of an abominable blindness. Such is
the apologetic significance of the character's allure, deliberately endowed
with every human quality—and, notably, the virtues—most appreciated in
our lay society.

Sombreval is described to us according to his own conscience, not
according to what can occur in his renegade priest's soul, that soul that he has
made only to alienate. And Barbey rightly makes this alienation the subject
of his book: he does not plumb the "subconscious" of the character, because
what we thereby name is translated in no other way than by the exterior facts
that are, nevertheless, only signs. But the abbot Sombreval, by having
thought to efface the indelible seal of the sacerdotal, sign of the holy sacrifice, would by this very fact be incapable of conceiving of the value of the
signs and *figures* that come to be produced around him, let alone be capable
of deciphering them.

Therefore everything that happens to him as events—the relations with
the other characters who arise in the course of his story—arise through his
own daughter Calixte, and he will interpret them; he will react according to
his scientific vision of existence, in an *erroneous* fashion.

The abbot Sombreval believes that he has abolished the illusory order
of a nonexistent providence with his apostasy. However, for the one who has
substituted for the mysteries of faith the representation of nature's secrets,
which it is the business of science to unveil, for the scholar who relies upon
his chemical experiments in order to determine "the movement of matter,"
as soon as he trusts in the natural laws within himself, which he has given
over to the most legitimate human tendencies, he appears frustrated by the

compensations that ought to assure him of the natural accomplishment of the *natural* act of reproduction. He never denies her paternity [*La paternité ne lui est point refusée*]. God does not destroy nature; on the contrary he makes it efficacious, in the same way that he never impedes the sinner in order never to impede the sinner's freedom [*pas plus qu'il n'empeche de pecher pour ne point empecher la liberte de pecher*]. Calixte, born "of the priest's woman," from the semen of a priest, enters the world with a birthmark, a cross marked on her brow, that incarnates the mystery rejected by the renegade priest. It is as though the sacramental seal of the violated priesthood was extended to the work of the flesh. Calixte becomes a young girl with a sublime beauty, afflicted with both somnambulism and catalepsy; the progeny of the abbot Sombreval is not normal at all and falls entirely within the demonic or angelic order. But how does Sombreval behave? In the most *natural*, most humane, but also the most passionate manner possible: that is to say with all the anxiety of a father who worries about his child. A mark of the genius of the author of the *Diaboliques* is that he even draws a mysterious lesson from his character's natural attitude. Sombreval, for all of his intrepid atheism, has nothing less than a god: Calixte. For all of his resources, he has nothing less than a ritual occupation: to look after his daughter. And with all of his science, he does not officiate over [*officie*] his laboratory except to sustain the *presence* of his mysteriously *absent* child— the opposite of *real presence*—tirelessly seeking the formula that ought to cure Calixte of the strange sickness that suspends her between life and death—which, for him, amounts to freeing her from his idea of vocation and redemption that he quite clearly blames for the apparent neurosis by which he sees her held. Is this to say that, being moved by his own fate, he ought to recoil before such a prodigious vexation, putting his initial resolution— his freedom, his choice—back into doubt? But the question cannot even be posed for him, because, between Calixte, who is a sign, and himself, there is the *prohibited paternity* that makes her this indecipherable sign. This is why Calixte, this fragile child, this secret Carmelite who prays day and night for the expiation of her accursed father, is also the rock, erected by Providence, against which Sombreval will break himself.

I will not linger here, following the details of the shocking turns that prepare his fall and that are caused by two circumstances: first the refusal of Calixte, bound by her secretly pronounced vows, to marry the young Néel of Néhou whose passion she exacerbates to the point of delirium,[iv] while Som-

---

iv. This hopeless love of young Néel for Calixte, the propitiatory virgin, forms without a doubt one of Barbey's most personal themes.

The desirable but unpossessable Calixte, whose beautiful body seems to have been created only to "transubstantiate" through suffering the too human emotions that it

breval stops at nothing in order to promote this love and the marriage that he hopes will be the surest means of curing Calixte's neurosis. Then comes the strange rumor of incest that begins to spread and which incites Sombreval to move away and then to resort to the sinister stratagem that precipitates the end of the story, with the dolorous and resigned complicity of young Néel.

---

inspires in the young man, an "absent presence" and then a "real presence" after which his carnal desire is purified and consumed—the fascination that she exercises over him almost makes him feel repugnance for his own fiancée—but above all the infinitely cruel scene where Calixte—already dying—reconciles him with his fiancée and obliges Néel to solemnly engage himself in the marriage—even though Néel has lost all taste for life; this entire ensemble of circumstances arises from what is for Barbey a Manichean representation, but that we have studied in Sade as a fundamental component of the sadist myth and *courtly love*. The idea of degeneration, of degradation, of impurity is linked, according to Sade, to the representation of a God who is the creator of necessarily impure creatures, leading to the degeneration of whatever it is attached to. From his atheism a notion of purity is developed—purity of the uncreated, purity of nothingness—a notion that is associated with the destruction of the sensible world, with the very *jouissance* of destroying, and that forms with destruction a singular absolute exigency: the sadist soul (as a creature itself) is attached to the loved object and preserves it only in order to destroy it, and thus develops its kind of self-cruelty.

The image of the virgin, of the chaste woman, symbol of the unpossessable celestial purity insofar as this symbol strikes virile covetousness with a curse, by its character becomes in itself cruelly provocative, the object of predilection upon which sadistic cruelty exercises itself in its representation up to the point of suspecting that the unviolated object—is violable. This is accursed virility's only assuagement for having wished to enjoy the unpossessable purity. But here this is only the replica of courtly love: here the image of the inviolate woman mortally wounds virility but excites it to the point of an adoration of celestial purity in the form of a creature. And nevertheless the adoration itself sustains the image of inviolate purity only by always reestablishing the contrary representation: unpossessable, purity is nonetheless violable in the creature that represents it. There still the lover, by a morose delectation counter to sadism, ceaselessly destroys the carnal form of purity, but immediately reconstitutes it by his very aspiration to possess unpossessable purity in the creature. In courtly love as in sadistic representation, this image of unpossessable purity excites virile energy to the point of *jouissance* by its accursedness. In order to thus portray the passion of young Néel for Calixte, which illustrates the theme of love for the unpossessable woman, Barbey described and then actualized what he had himself experienced in his adolescence. Without a doubt his passion, when he was thirty years old, for the young daughter of his cousin Edelstand du Méril, the beautiful Ernestine of whom he says that having helped her into the saddle, he embraced the knees of the young Amazon with all the ardor that, much later, he remembered as the most intense kiss that he had ever given. But one of the greatest reverberations in his adolescent soul was the experience that he recounts to Trébutien as follows: "I am actually born on the *day of deaths*, at two in the morning, a wretched time [*par un temps du Diable*]. I have come as Romulus has gone—in a tempest. Like Fontenelle, I failed to die an hour or two after my birth, but there are good reasons why I may die before I am one hundred years old. Apparently the umbilical cord was badly knotted and as my blood carried my life away into the blankets of my crib, a

With what intention has the author insinuated this rumor that imputes incest to the couple of the accursed father and his daughter, the chaste Calixte? This is certainly not a simple turning point in the action, and I would venture to say that Barbey, throughout the development of the plot, had already thought of it, even choosing a propitious moment to make this simple episode intervene as one of the unforeseeable paths of Providence that is, in fact, nothing other than a *provocation* for Sombreval's benefit. If it seems episodic—and its value only becomes clear with the "scenario" of the denouement—the inconceivable rumor has above all the value of those signs that Sombreval does not notice at all; he takes it as a pure and simple slander whose absurdity and odiousness scandalize him, less for his own sake than for Calixte. By wanting to justify the human against God, nature against the supernatural, the norms of reason against mystery—this is the apologetic significance of this episode—Sombreval has lost the means of justifying himself before men, even though he is completely natural, reasonable, normal, and human. Now this God, contrary to nature and reason, reclaims him once again, him, the man "set apart." But, through the device of the slanderous rumor, he now speaks of him in an equivocal language of a such a kind that, by the defamatory accusation of incest, one sees Sombreval, this man of integrity, suffering doubly in his honor and his paternal love: the chastity of his daughter Calixte, the servant of that God "contrary to nature," is placed in doubt. There where Sombreval is surrendered not only to the most human but to the most legitimate inclination, he suddenly appears as a father denatured by a corrupt young girl. It is of little concern to Sombreval to find himself charged with all these crimes by a superstitious populace; but it is because he has an innate sense of justice, because he fears that this slander will be mortal for Calixte, that he decides to tear himself from Calixte—and to make Calixte tear herself from him—and all in order to have reacted not as a denatured, but simply as a human father.

The couple of Sombreval and his daughter Calixte, living in the heart of a general outcry, like pariahs folded over upon each other, in their battle for and against one another—seeing them now accused of incest, how can we

---

woman (my first *secret* love as an adolescent), a friend of my mother, noticed that I was pale and saved me not from the Waters, like Moses, but from Blood—another flow in which I would have perished. Destiny is remarkable [*singulière*]! A woman saved me so that I might love her *thirty years* later with that inflamed timidity that is the most terrible malady that I know. . . . Is this a charm redoubled by the distant days of infancy? But this woman, now old, and who has never known anything of the ardors that she has caused me, and by which, physically, I failed to die, I have not seen her again since my departure for college, and I have never since found, *under a beloved brow*, the somber blue look of the wrathful falcon that might reward me with that imperious and fiery look!" *Lettres à Trébutien*, v. 2, pp. 184–185, letter dated October 1, 1851.

not think here of the same formation of the father and the daughter in Sade's *Eugénie de Franval?*[11] There we have the portrait of an incest consummated, but, from the beginning, by a deliberately monstrous couple compared to Sombreval and Calixte: Eugénie, not only her atheist father's lover, but also his docile disciple, and Franval who pushes his daughter's corruption to the point of her mother's murder. And nevertheless, Franval displays the same jealous fervor for preserving his daughter from debauchery, he possesses the same anxiety to shield Eugénie from family and marriage plans, as Sombreval does to conserve Calixte's life in the hopes of marrying her to young Néel. But each of the atheists avows in almost the same terms that they have only one religion, one god: their daughters. Is this pure coincidence? In *Eugénie de Franval* the incestuous father is precipitated into the inextricable following a discussion with a priest, while in *A Married Priest* it is after the parish priest approaches Sombreval in order to try to separate him from his daughter, in order to put an end to the odious rumor, that Sombreval decides to resort to the final stratagem. It is not without interest to follow for a moment the strange similarities that, in their very dissimilarity, frame Barbey's novel and Sade's story. This approximation allows one ultimately to extricate a structural affinity between the two characters, their interior dispositions regarding atheism, and their respectively divergent reactions in the face of incest, inherent to fatherhood. Franval invokes atheism—like all of Sade's heroes, who do so under the pretext of legitimating their acts—in order to freely abandon himself to incest. On the other hand, the abbot Sombreval only knows marriage, widowerhood, and fatherhood by having become an atheist. Each character tramples the divine law underfoot, but while Franval knowingly destroys the familial institutions by claiming incest as a privilege of fatherhood, Sombreval instead calls on those institutions as a human privilege that he wants to establish on the ruins of religion. Franval is only a pervert, jealous to the point of destroying his own family; Sombreval is so totally lacking in perversity that the mere idea that one could suspect Calixte's purity inspires in him such a profound horror that it is precisely this horror of vice that leads (as we learn) to murder, to the real consummation of his sacrilege and, finally, to suicide, following the example of Franval. Thus two works of opposed inspiration conclude with an identical denouement. What does this prove? that the two authors, like their characters, support each other back to back with their differently expressed affinities [*du fait de leurs affinities, différemment exprimées*]; knowing the nothingness of morality. The measure of the full reversal of principles effectuated since Sade can be taken from this parallel between *Eugénie de Franval* and *A Married Priest*: according to him, Franval rebels and fights with the violence of his incestuous passion against a divinity that is still completely rational, imprinted on social institutions as well as in the norms of human nature. God is certainly on the side of reason, and the godless man is on the side of obscure forces. In Barbey d'Aurevilly one finds a total upheaval of the relations of man with God; this is because, in the interval, there was Joseph de Maistre; the argument of authority subordinates reason: it is nothing other than a persuasive way of arguing that all of existence arises from a hidden and incomprehensible God; his language is that of catastrophe and crimes, not virtue and prosperity. And from now on the action of the divine power that appears in the *Married Priest* seems, to the eyes of reason, more and more complicit with madness and the transgression of laws, insofar as it sets human nature outside of itself and holds common sense in contempt.

A remarkable thing, but one that completes his portrayal of the character of the renegade priest, Sombreval, is that although he is incapable of deciphering the *signs* regarding himself, nonetheless he grasps the meaning of the *value* of these signs for his own daughter. What's more, he respects Calixte's piety but in the manner of a sane man before the delirium of a loved one; it is the fear of losing her that inspires this respect in him. He thus sets out to win back again to life this child that a religion, detestable to his eyes, disputes with him, borrowing from the *world of signs*, which is Calixte's, a last chance to cure her, in other words using *sympathetic magic* in order to "disenchant" his daughter's soul. He will perform all of the gestures of piety, of repentance: he will go to make honorable amends before the bishop and, in his penitential retreat, he will again celebrate the holy Mass. Calixte can then believe that her prayer is answered and, seeing her father finally touched by grace, she will consider herself freed from her vows and she will marry Néel. For the happiness of his daughter Sombreval will sacrifice his firm conviction upon which all the probity of his conscience rests: the nonexistence of God. . . . Here the properly inquisitorial nature of Barbey's psychology appears: however little it matters to Sombreval to mock a nonexistent God, through paternal love he comes to mock himself. Ultimately, he renounces himself. But Sombreval does not even believe in his own truth. As though divine justice had waited for precisely this moment in order to execute the sentence that was suspended up to now, the celestial punishment immediately crushes the impostor priest. At the announcement of her father's conversion, Calixte's joy is so strong that she is plunged into the worst of crises. In her cataleptic state, Calixte has a vision of her father's abomination. She dies from it. Warned too late, and returning to his daughter's grave, nothing more remains for Sombreval, racked by the most furious madness, but to unearth Calixte and to throw himself into the pond of his manor along with her corpse.

A denouement so rigorously logical in its savage grandeur—but so paradoxical in the cruelty of its apologetic intention—that it can only scandalize right-thinking liberal Catholics. The apparently "useless" sacrifice of Calixte, along with the sufferings sustained by young Néel, that hold the reader breathless throughout the entire story [*recit*], the grace refused to the accursed priest: in this entire story, what became of the dogma of the reversibility of the innocent's merits in favor of the guilty? Why does this end appear so true to us? Why do the *motifs* invoked seem so false?

Such a question would seem completely vain if one didn't persist in taking this book literally and trying to find its edifying value. In order to dispose of this illusion—which was perhaps the author's own—it is appropriate to consider the difficulties that one is sure to have in trying to grasp any novelist who proposes a thesis, for the very good [*forte*] reason that every novelist is an apologist. Barbey, in effect, never stops underlining many circumstances that ultimately support dogma, both circumstances of divine prescience as well as those fundamental ones of atonement. However, these two aspects immediately awaken the conflict, insoluble for reason, of the coincidence of grace and the freedom of the will, and we will see that Barbey, led by the movement proper to his creation, perhaps thereby surpasses his own intention. However, if he wanted "to demonstrate" something, he has demonstrated the powerlessness of free wills to act upon each other. Why does Calixte, despite her holocaust, seem to be able to do nothing against the malediction that leads her father to suicide, any more than Sombreval was able to bring Calixte to yield to young Néel? *There are many things that the saints want to see produced by the saintly will inspired by God, but that nevertheless will not be produced, even though they pray for certain things with piety and in a saintly manner; but God never does what they pray him to do, rather by his Holy Spirit he himself makes in them this will to pray. And when the saints will and pray to God that everyone should be saved, we can say: "God wills it and does not do it," in the sense that we say he himself wills who makes them will in such a way.* Is this to say that God does not answer the prayer for the salvation of each and every person that he inspires in the saints? This concerns the prescience by which God has foreknowledge that a particular man will want or will not want to sin. Saint Augustine does not at all mean that this divine prescience *can shackle the free will of man. Therefore it is not at all because God has foreknowledge of the future that nothing belongs to our will. For God does not have foreknowledge of a pure absence of will. But if God, who knows what will be in our will in the future, does not know a simple absence of will, but something real, this is because there is, by the fact of divine foreknowledge, something that depends on our will. . . . For this reason, equally, objurgations, vituperations, praises and exhortations are no more vain than laws, since God has foreseen that they would be, and* they act strongly *only because God foresees their efficacity. . . . Man never sins because God has foreknowledge that he will sin; on the contrary we can hardly doubt that he sins because that one whose foreknowledge is never in error, knows, not by fate, chance, or by anything else but by this very man that he will sin. This man, if he does not will it, will never sin; but, in this case, God foresees that he will never sin.*[v]

---

v. Saint Augustine, *The City of God*, XXII, c. 2.

This is certainly not the place to debate the extent to which Saint Augustine's proposition settles the conflict and might not allow a nuance of predestination to subsist even apart from divine prescience. At the very least, if it has been settled in these terms, it is in the sense of the freedom, and therefore also of the absolute responsibility of man in the absolute power he has of resisting grace. Henceforth, in Sombreval's case, *Calixte can do nothing against her father's freedom* which leads him to damnation. But Sombreval, the impenitent atheist, never knows anything of his damnation since, if he commits suicide, it is because he damns himself in the absence of a God who would damn him.

Correctly understood, Saint Augustine's argument should not serve here to "explicate" the true meaning of Barbey's novel. Upon reflection it can clarify for us how such a capital proposition of Christian dogma is here found mythologized in the action imagined by a great Catholic novelist who, out of concern for his creation, isolates an aspect of the dogma at the expense of a coherent dogmatic whole [*ensemble*]. One then discovers a machinery that, though it seems completely contradictory from the point of view of the doctrine by which it claims to be inspired, is nevertheless obedient to the preoccupations of an entirely different order in a more profound way than even the author suspects. The trap for an apologist author resides in *making* Providence *speak* while *doubling* it, as he necessarily substitutes for it the entire length of his story [*recit*]. Any one of Balzac's great novels can be much more convincingly interpreted in an "apologetic" sense because he had no pretension to this genre at all. The Russians are the ones who, in order to leave the field free for divine grace, do not breathe a word on this subject but apply themselves to lamenting the degeneration of their characters with an infinite compassion. Obviously nothing of this sort is found in Barbey. There is only a morose delectation for the ineluctable that responds simultaneously to a polemical ardor and to a taste for the spectacular. Certainly we owe to this taste for the spectacular a character such as the "great Malgaigne." The figure of this old weaver performs a contradictory function in the book: a sorceress, but converted, she gives the action the tone of a folklore legend, at the same time that she *personifies* divine prescience by her gift of seeing. She seems immediately to change the entire religious perspective of the book: it is one thing to describe this freedom that God gives to man out of which a Balzac or a Dostoevsky constitute the vertigo of their heroes, it is something else to express through the organ of a character that God has foreknowledge of the secret of the characters depicted [*mis en scene*]. What the Church Father wants to prevent in the not-very-confident minds [*consciences mal assurées*] of the pagan neophytes—the confusion between divine prescience and fate [*fatum*]—is here reestablished by the novelist. And it is certainly in the nature of things, all the more so since, in a poetic creation, we truthfully know nothing of what God knows or wants, nor even of what the poet's own fate [*fatalité*] wants and knows. Through this character of the weaver, who comes onto the scene at the beginning and looms up at every new turn to announce the irremediable or the irremissable, Barbey has actually described the *powerlessness*, in the very prescience of the future, *of intervening in the destiny of beings*, a powerlessness proper to the gods of ancient paganism, proper to poets who take up events and characters and who can otherwise only *celebrate* or *transfigure* them. Sorceress and seer, the great Malgaigne reflects the fascination with *Fate* that the novelist sets himself to unraveling with his story: beings and things are what they are, and there is kindness in representing them in that way—a polemical kindness before the progressive superstition of a detested century—an interior kindness in the most profound, but also the most nostalgic pessimism. Whether the divinity is essentially cruel (Sombreval) or infinitely loving and sad (Calixte and Néel), it remains the case that in *A Married Priest* all the positions are absolute and irreducible: that of Calixte, of Néel, of Sombreval, and of God. *They can do nothing for one another.*

Such is, viewed from within, this *Castle of the Bellows, which* Barbey wants *you to be interested in as in a person.*

And ultimately the figure of Sombreval, in his renegade's isolation, braving superstition, illustrates well the poet's isolation at the heart of the world of *utility* in which he lives—damned—upon the "products" of his delirium, "products" without either price or exchange value, nothing but sin: the atheist's sacrilege can have no value in the "economy of salvation" that rejects him as the poet rejects the economy of utility—a paradoxical homage rendered to the *Precious Blood* that has no price at all. . . .

I am possessed by the same subject. I sing in my register and in my chords.

There is a more muted aspiration perceptible here: a return to the mythic images that recovers a story [recit] in which language must simultaneously illustrate the customs of a milieu, of a region, and the obscure forces that haunt it—antagonistic or allied forces that the author rediscovers in his own reverie as though in an exploration of places from his childhood: here and there these forces are always fighting according to a hidden justice. For a moment they have assumed the physiognomy of the characters of an action and are detached from their legendary ground, and the apologist, according to what flatters or repulses the author's impulses, translates their conflict into the terms of sacrilege and expiation. But beneath the mask of characters, what these forces by themselves have of the inexpiable or inexorable upsets the apologetic argument in their favor, and soon these forces are reabsorbed within the proper movement of the legend. The importance of passage and the dreamy description of places testifies to this attraction of the fatality properly inherent to the cadence of natural phenomena: the sea, the night, the settings of the sun, the shadow of the forests, auroras, twilights: the spectral figure of Calixte is slowly effaced by the morning, like that of Sombreval vanishing in the waters of his pond. The physiognomies of places and characters are therefore in a perfect interdependence. Both ultimately provide an account of a state of the soul overcome by the legend whose fatality ought to be recounted, and of the soul's need to hear it as its own melody. It is fitting that the entire story is narrated on *a balcony overlooking the Seine* by this Rollon Langrune, whose mere name is revealing in its origin. Barbey writes to Trébutien: "You have no place in your Caen a shore of Langrune which does not lack character [*physionomie*], and one year I made fly there a ship like that which set Phaedra to dreaming! Phaedra was not nearby. Nothing showed, nothing was sent to me by Neptune, who was that day a soft and charming cerulean, *blue-booted*, Trébutien, and I returned to Caen without being crushed. . . . That is all that I saw of your Langrune, but I now need to know what this word "Langrune" means in old Normandy patois—in the old Normandy language. In German, *Langrune* means *green* earth. The shore of Langrune has a number of plants, dune plants—but in saying "Langrune," our fathers the pirates, those *Earthless Johns* [*Jean sans Terre*] who had no other lord than the sea, did they not mean the sea, which was the earth for them—their *green earth?*"[12]

Chapter Five

The Mass of Georges Bataille

A PROPOS OF *L'ABBÉ C.*[i]

This book is *impious* and that is why it had to be written.

Nothing is more vain than to allow only expressions that reassure or sat-isfy consciences. The proverb that claims "silence is golden" has dubious con-sequences in the realm of acts. One must counter this proverb by holding that if acts must be pure, silence must be pure as well; that silence is never pure if words break its continuity with acts; that, acts obeying silence, words are spo-ken only in order to hide this obedience, either for good or for evil.

How could the purity of silence be obtained if speech never uttered the things that are constantly born in silence, because speech vouches for this purity? And yet this purity is nothing, no more than is a heart which would be called [*s'affirmerait*] pure, even if it inspired words. Purity belongs to silence alone and thereby to the absence of the speakable. Purity has never appeared; and whenever it has been palpably and visibly shown it has suffered the torture intended for "treason" and thus for words; this torture proves that no matter how visible it is, it nonetheless retains the purity that belongs only to silence. (Your speech is: no—no, yes—yes, the rest is the Devil's.) But for there to be a pure silence—since it seems that purity and silence are absolutely identical—there must also be a speech that must be impure for there to be a speech that is pure. An impure silence yields a speech that in order to be pure is not truly speech, but is laden with silence, and, what is worse, with an impure and false silence. A Rhenish mystic said that a soul that contains this false silence is anguished because it is *out of place*. It is not in that through which it is. It wants *to be* and not to rest in that through

---

i. Georges Bataille, *L'Abbé C.* (Paris: Éditions de Minuit, 1950).

ii. *The Gay Science*, Book 3, §143 (Klossowski cites §141), p. 191.

which it is. It imagines a number of perishable things all the more zealously because it delights in the mere fact of perishing. It must certainly perish in order to rest in that through which it is, but it delights only in wasting away, not in the attraction of that through which it is, which is precisely the authentic silence within it. So says the master of the Rhenish mystics.[1] This soul speaks in order not to be in its place but exclusively in its words. Its words must convince it of a silence that it does not have. It says very beautiful things; it speaks of virtues, laws, of renouncing itself out of love for its silence and its neighbor. But it speaks more, and the neighbor is less touched by what it says: since he is the neighbor, he rightly knows only the true silence and knows that it cannot be attained by the soul's good deeds unless the "works" truly unfurl from this soul's pure silence and not from its words.

The soul must therefore expel everything that it silently imagines: it is only for the price of an *impure speech* that the soul can hope *to rest in silence*, in the silence through which it is, being itself nothing more than this silence. If the soul must perish in order to become this, it perishes [*parvient à périr*] only by speaking. For insofar as it perishes, it must renounce itself, and it will renounce itself only by *renouncing the purity of its words*. If someone tells us that a soul that rests in that through which it is—in its silence—must necessarily communicate to another the silence that it "enjoys," that it therefore has recourse to speech, and that this speech is necessarily pure, we will then ask how, if it rests in the *silence* through which it is, the need to speak still arises in it if not from the fact that it never rests in silence at all; if the soul speaks, it must say the opposite in order to attain this silence and if it speaks of it, then not only is it not in the silence, but it is horrified by it. Whoever has ever so slightly reflected on these things, unless he has rediscovered them through a need to speak, will understand that he cannot have a *pure* language, let alone [*à plus forte raison*] a pious language, let alone [*à plus forte raison*] a language that could pronounce the *ultimate questions* by means of common sense, without immediately provoking—both in the one who speaks and in the one who listens—either *an impossibility of silence*, or an impure and false silence. To say impure things, under the pretext of finding a pure silence within oneself—who would dare to envy such a condition? Who has ever experienced such torture? Those who blaspheme are only aiming to offer the spectacle of indignation to others, but they fool themselves since they prize this indignation *for nothing*.

The first to be enraged by this, the first to be wounded by the images born in his intimate silence, is Georges Bataille. This is why he must write "wounding" books, but that wound only those who have confidence in what they say and who are taken at their word. Is this not their business? If they are convinced, so be it! But why then are they uncomfortable? Is it because the very language that each one of them uses and is so sure of can disturb those that they have convinced once it is allowable to turn it back against the truth that they proclaim? Is this not rather the proof that truth offers against all language?

An impure silence that corrects a pure language—an impious silence that is chastised by pious words—and on the other hand a pure silence that can be discovered only by an impious or obscene language—this fact is at the origin of a book as wounding, as shocking, as impious as the story of *L'Abbé C.*; at the same time, it is the very subject matter of the book.

Georges Bataille has this in common with Sade: for him pornography is a form of the spirit's battle against the flesh, a form that is thereby determined by atheism, because if there is no God who created the flesh, then there are no longer those excesses of language residing in the spirit that aim to reduce the excesses of the flesh to silence. Thus, there is nothing more "verbal" than the excesses of the flesh. In Sade language does not wind up exhausting itself, intolerable to itself, after relentlessly setting itself upon the same victim for days at a time. Language is condemned to an endless reiteration. In Bataille, separated from the apparent rationalism of Sade by more than a century of Hegelian reflections, the identification of language and transgression is intensified. The carnal act is attractive only and precisely if it is a transgression of language by the flesh and of the flesh by language. This transgression is lived as ecstasy; if the flesh truly knows [*connaît bien*] ecstasy in orgasm, this ecstasy is nothing compared to the *spiritual orgasm* which, in fact, is only the consciousness of an event, but one that is *past* at the very moment when the mind believes that it grasps it in speech. However, there can be no transgression in the carnal act if it is not lived as a spiritual event, but in order to grasp the object within it, one must seek out and *reproduce* the event in a reiterated description of the *carnal act*. This reiterated description of the carnal act not only provides an account of transgression, it is itself a transgression of language by language.

Understood correctly, this is not merely a question of an ethical transgression, but of the violence done to the integrity of a being by something that appears to the mind [*l'esprit*] only in the being's disintegration—thus there is less of a need to do bad in spite of the imperative to do good, than of a need *to make what is beautiful, ugly*—by disfiguring a face, for example, or corrupting what appears pure. This something that then appears to the mind is by nature *capable of adoration* [*adorable*]; it is either something that overcomes the mind, or it is the very state of adoration in which the mind then finds itself. But if everything passes [*tout passe*] in language, adoration itself escapes from it. Sade denied the "objective" reality of sacrilege and recognized it as having only an erogenous value; but his imagination could not go further than this because in order to appreciate it as erogenous he reestablished it in its objectivity through the simple fact of speaking or writing. The example of Bataille proves it again: every process takes its point of departure from this irreducible experience; for him sacrilege has an "ontological" function; in the act of profaning *the most noble name* of existence, *its presence* is revealed. Thus Bataille, despite his athe-ist attitude, remains in solidarity with the whole Christian cultural structure. The *priest*, the *mass*, the *sacraments*, all the accessories of the cult, even the *name of God*, are indispensable for Bataille's *expression*. One can certainly say that these are the proper elements of a language that provides an account—according to conditions of comprehension determined by Catholic habits—of an experience that otherwise cannot be explicated; but if Bataille had the means to translate his experience in another way, I strongly doubt that he would want to be deprived of the means that precisely provide him with the mental structures of the Church.

The *words of consecration* with which the priest converts the substance of the bread and wine into the substance of the flesh and blood of the Savior—separating them completely by their succession (he consecrates first *the body*, then *the blood*) the body and the blood—nevertheless establish the divine flesh and blood in the abolition of the substances of the bread and the wine. Manifest in the abolition of the species [*espèces*] of the bread and the wine, the *real presence* of the *Savior* itself appears only *in the separation of his body and his blood; it is under the form* [*sous la figure*] *of his death that the Savior is really present.* The Catholic dogma of transubstantiation thus demonstrates how the sacrifice on the cross, accomplished once and for all, is nonetheless present in time and can be reiterated as an *actual* sacrifice. One sees immediately how the dogma of the real presence, with all of the mental operations that it sup-poses, provides the material for wild, sacrilegious imaginings: by allowing God to be made present, but veiled under the species of a food, thus of an object, consecration exposes the divine presence to every possible injury—in the same way that one would strip a human body. Certainly the real presence in the Holy Sacrament is, in the theological sense, realized by the believer as an interior event, and the space where the encounter of the believer and the divine presence is situated is a spiritual space. Nonetheless the consecrated host acts independently of the degree of belief or disbelief of the assistants or communicants. The real presence is therefore not subjective at all, but objec-tive—God is there, exposed to the eyes—it is certainly him veiled under the species of the bread and the wine—but it is this very veil, this veil of his death, that forms the separation of his body and his blood—that makes it pre-sent and exposes it, in the same way that the nudity of a body exposes it to outrages. The *rapprochement* between the real presence of God and the nudity of a human being immediately imposes itself; what is shocking is that, with-out speaking here of the "black" traditions of minds like Sade and Bataille, they are at work as though in an impossible meditation.

The existence of the priest, of the man who consecrates the bread and wine to the body and blood of the Son of God, but who, for this action, has taken a vow of chastity and who consequently represents within himself the separation of the body and soul—this existence constitutes for Bataille's mind both a perpetual menace and a provocation. If such is the mystery of being, if such is the form of this mystery—then Bataille's attitude would be vain insofar as it tends to abolish this form. But, on the contrary, it retains all its value for Bataille to the extent that, by his own contestation, he strives to give an account of the non-apparent content of this mystery to which, with the same gesture, he adheres completely [il n'en adhère pas moins pleinement]. Ultimately, if the sacerdotal and sacramental form of the mystery retains what is abolished by its visible ritual operation, Bataille's attitude aspires to reestablish—by means of language—what the ritual operation destroys by abandoning it to silence. One then witnesses a reprise of the mental operations that are a prelude to the *real presence* in favor of what these operations abolish. What consecration abolishes in the profound meaning of the transubstantiation are—under the form of the bread and wine—the *transgressions* of the flesh, since its desires are what were nailed upon the cross. What consecration establishes is the heavenly flesh within the divine presence. But this is because, for Bataille, transgression in the carnal act has the same value as a kind of inverse transubstantiation: because all intact "flesh" is effectively experienced by Bataille as already "heavenly," profanation becomes a spiritual force.

But from where does the profaning transgression (lived in the carnal act) draw its virtue of transubstantiation if not from the eminent fact that, through the words of consecration, the mind has abolished the carnal desires; through the mind's words of death the abolished flesh attains the real presence of heavenly flesh. In Bataille's mind something of the heavenly flesh is confounded with what he calls the being's integrity, particularly with the integrity of all flesh—and all intact flesh has something analogous to heavenly flesh. But this very integrity carries in itself the profanation, the violence that can be done to it, since it is in the menacing relation to the disintegrating act of profanation that the mind conceives of integrity. What's more, without this menace suspended over "intact flesh," integrity would not be experienced by the mind at all. *Intact*, the other's flesh appears as a symbol of its own death—death of the carnal life—but also as *presence* beyond death, but if it bears the menace of profanation as constitutive of its integrity, this means that there is profanation itself in this presence. This *presence* immediately ceases to have a transcendental reality; in relation to that menace of profanation that now fixes the mind, it is nothing more than an immanent reality, like the species in relation to the consecratory words, and this happens through the profaning act, through the violation that works the inverted transubstantiation. The difficulty of describing this aberration arises because it can be only discursively, since it is produced in an instantaneous similitude between ritual transubstantiation and opposition to the rite, and always as its inversion. *Similitude* in the sense that, in the sort of pathological ecstasy that would obtain, for example, the profanation of the host, the real

presence that is then revealed is exactly the same as what is revealed in adoration, but *opposition* in the sense that what is then adored is the destructive
operation of the mind. Adoration limits the mind by real presence, by the
presence of the other; the profanation of the host abolishes the mind's limits
which is why this kind of ecstasy is identical to the orgasm that is experienced
as a suppression of the body's limits; but the inverted "transubstantiation" that
the profaning spirit thus works upon "heavenly flesh" as if it were mere material, only an immanent thing, is only a simulacrum of language insofar as it is
also the same transcendence that the mind seeks. It is a simulacrum that is also
evident in the transgression experienced in the carnal act: does the transgressive spirit not ultimately seek there to transubstantiate what it desires, the *abolition* of the carnal limits experienced in orgasm? Does the violent act by which
a body is *stripped* not represent *the abolition* of the very *person* that one strips?
What is revealed by this *destruction*, whether physical or moral, is then a real
presence that cannot be known or retained, an ecstasy where *the mind is somehow contemplated outside of itself*, where it attempts to grasp its spoils [*larcin*] in
the "abolition" of its supreme state; but this "abolition" can only operate as a
simulacrum. And this simulacrum is perhaps his worst plunder [*pire larcin*].
One could say that Bataille cannot do without the *name of God* any more than
a priest can do without the bread and wine for consecration. However, for the
priest, as soon as the bread and wine are the *flesh* and *blood of the Savior, bread*
and *wine* are no more than *inappropriate words*. The same is true, for Bataille,
of the *name of God* which is in some way the material of a *counter-sacrament*,
by which [*sur laquelle*] the mind only acts upon itself in order to destroy itself;
a destruction whose illusion is provided by the intense shock that it suffers in
the verbal insurrection against the very thing that nonetheless remains the
sign of its supreme identity: *the name of God*.

Chapter Six

Language, Silence, and Communism

Parain is a teacher. His philosophy—which is much too restrained in dealing with colorful insinuations because it is too well informed about the evils that it combats—is addressed to the most humanly urgent part of each of us in the situation that contemporary history makes for us: our need for truth which, for him, remains inseparable from our will to live. His thought would certainly be more direct, and more immediately accessible, if it did not willingly side with all of our paradoxes—paradoxes that it must reproduce and reconstruct in order to then lead us to disarticulate the false structures within which we have entrapped ourselves. For this reason alone his investigations on language are nothing less than free gifts; whatever objections they arouse through the prin-ciple of their orientation, they are especially meaningful in a social milieu where the fact of speaking, the love of formulas, has become more than a mere vice; indeed it is a veritable sickness, a menace to everyone's body and soul.

Ultimately Parain's concern, at the level of the individual man, goes right to the flesh; less to the soul than to the flesh that speaks, to all of the vicissitudes that arise from the association of speech [*la parole*] and the flesh, especially as the soul tends to dissociate language [*le langage*] from the flesh, forgetting that it is in and through the flesh that it must render an account to truth. In his battles against the adversary, Parain often evokes old Tertul-lian from his battle against the Docetes.[1] This is what leads Parain to refer constantly to the dogma of the Resurrection of the flesh that is the alpha and omega of his thought [*qui demeure le commencement et la fin de toutes les démarches de sa pensée*]. This argument, which in the eyes of unbelieving thought holds only as a postulate, disposes Parain to understand—if not to sympathize with—those very people who today appear as the most zealous detractors of Christianity.

Parain has lived in Russia, with its Bolshevik experience grafted onto the "carnal" Christianity of the Russian people, and this remains for him not only his determinant personal experience but also the crucial event in light of which he sets about weighing and measuring everything that we in the West are inclined to oppose to the communist experience. We will see later why Parain calls it the place of silence.

Parain's attitude of waiting in the face of communism is the same patience that the Russian man possesses; whether by agreement or force, who knows whether Bolshevist materialism might not be in the process— contrary to its own statements—of giving Christianity the body that will replace the already weak Western one? "The spirit is in the world not only in order to affirm the idea, but in order to give it a body. This body cannot be that of someone tortured. It can only be a glorious body. Christianity and communism are in agreement on this point, even as they define glory differently."[i] "In 1903 . . . the Bolshevik party in Russia, by requiring its members to completely renounce any activity other than that of fighting for the proletarian revolution, founded the first modern monastic order. This is how the religious revolution of our era began. It has also restored the rule of ideas by stating at the same time that there is effective action only when it conforms to a firmly and previously established theory."[ii] "The first modern Councils were the Russian Soviets.[iii] "Communism teaches us again one of the fundamental principles of traditional philosophy: that the individual is a being that is subordinate to the law of language, that is to say to the law of ideas. But the idea is properly the first degree of man's ascension toward God."[2]

The *intelligentzia* of our generation in France is currently swept up in an ever more frantic questioning of the reality of this world and devotes itself to an incantation of absence—not that of a world absent from this one, but of an *absence of the world* from things and beings—by means of language. In France, however—a portrait of a society threatened by complete proletarianization— the official teaching can only favor this requestioning because, as Parain says, this teaching, which consists in affirming that there is no truth, denies the very principle of teaching. To society's implicit nihilism this explicit one responds with a literature all the more clever for identifying language with the discontinuity and informality with which it masks its misery, which is nothing other than everyone's misery, giving an arbitrary word [*parole*] to a quiet distress *that has no name*. Today the names of things and beings no longer really belong to them in a legitimate way and seem to correspond to them only more or less arbitrarily: by weariness according to some, usurpation

---

i. Brice Parain, *L'Embarras du choix* (Paris: Gallimard, 1946), p. 100.
ii. Ibid., p. 115.
iii. Ibid., p. 117.

according to others. Again it seems that anonymity would be the most advan-
tageous thing for the greatest good of all: liberty.

Moreover, this is what guides our contemporary metaphysics which
teaches thinking (about) existence by suppressing "the most noble name"
that language has given to it, thus suggesting that existence and language
have no other origin than consciousness itself, which is henceforth free to
limit or to extend its action according to self-created criteria.

The thought of Brice Parain is disconcerting first of all because it is centered
upon some infinitely simple truths and because, almost immediately, even
before they are told to us, it offers an account of the impossibility of stating
them in a direct way: he must follow the path of error to the end where we
completely lost these truths.

The first [of these simple truths] is that man does not exist without language
because language has created him; the second is that in order to fulfill his purpose or simply to maintain his current state, he must perform his acts in solidarity with his speech; finally, the third is that as soon as he transgresses the speech
"of his mouth," he destroys his existence and abandons his human specificity.

However, this transgression can be produced in two different senses:
either it is a matter of a devalorization of speech by existence and by the simultaneous requestioning of speech and existence in the search for an experience
without solution [sans issu], or it is a matter of a devalorization of existence by
a speech, separated from existence, that takes the place of experience.

Parain's new reflections on language and existence can be read as objections to
the critique to which Sartre has subjected his analyses of language.[iv] According
to Sartre, for there to be a problem of language, the Other must be given first.
Language is nothing but existence in the presence of others. However, language
is identified here with the judgment of others by which we become an object;
others alienate us by their judgments, which we feel set upon us. And he concludes, against Parain, that one must maintain the priority of the cogito, of the
"universalizing syntheses," of the immediate experience of others.[v]

Again, Parain maintains the priority of language in the face of and against
every myth of the transcendental ego.

If individual consciousness plays the role of an absolute beginning—as it
does for phenomenology—then it is hardly capable of anything but the passive

---

iv. J-P Sartre, Situations I, "Aller et Retour" (Paris: Gallimard, 1947), pp. 189–244.
[Sartre's essay is an extended critical review of Parain's Recherches sur la nature et les functions du langage.—trans.]

v. Ibid., p. 238.

contemplation of an eternal peace: thus, says Parain, each time that peace is troubled it has the feeling of the absurd. Ultimately, inertia being the law of this consciousness, it does not know how to describe any of the events that grip us and suspend our reflection: births, deaths, acts of violence, revolts, suicides, social crises, wars. But our anxieties [angoisses], our revolts, our doubt, which are so many suspensions of judgment, reveal on the contrary moments of rupture and instability. If consciousness "were an unbroken whole [ensemble], it would persevere in its constitutive syntheses of objects."[3] "On the contrary, the intervention of speech strips the character of finitude from every event of our existence. With language we enter, for better or worse, the order of the indefinite if not the infinite."[4] Given the fact of language, our existence is powerless to dispose either of its death or of its life.

Every act of our existence, for Parain, even the simplest breath, is a judgment that introduces a value into the world. Upon reflection, every thought is exercised only through the suspension of judgment. If, for example, I hold my breath and my speech, then there is the possibility of rupture; and if I am then free to be quiet or to speak, it is between silence and speech, not one speech or another. However, I notice further that I do not think of anything that I do not end up naming. Aside from tragic moments, everything always results in an explication, and if I do not speak, others will speak in my place: this is the law of our accomplishment and of the culture of every society. Thus, for Parain, being is synonymous with being said.

But precisely in the tragic moments, or those simply made grievous by our doubt, our contingency is revealed and with it comes revolt. As I imagine myself freely enjoying my existence as a plenitude before being satisfied in the silence of a created creature, suddenly there is something for me—no longer a master of intervening but now subject to the operation of responding—to explain. Better: if I *say* it, I will cease to be, because I cannot be happy all alone. Freedom must be taught because it is not free, says Parain. This means that I lose my freedom because I am obliged to speak and I can only hope to find it again beyond my speech. I affirm something, and I reproach myself immediately for saying too much—this is already nothing but a negation, says Parain who again here rejoins Blanchot: *for what is does not have to be and I remove its being from it by attributing it to it.* Thus I am only a means of language for making come to be that which is not yet.

Parain determines that he has here attained the place from which one can perceive the double defect common to transcendental idealism and Cartesian idealism. They have situated the suspension of judgment at the moment the first word is uttered. However, I suspend my judgment "after breathing and walking, at the precise moment when, receiving my first impression of the exterior world, I decide to name it."[5] Because every impression and every emotion is my part of the world, this part is too heavy for me to be capable of taking on all alone. This is because this part of the world assimilates me to universal necessity; it establishes me in the carnal community of my fellow men. But barely have I spoken, than I find myself separated from necessity and equality simultaneously: "I command or implore, I establish inequality, placing myself above or below the level of the common."[6] Having spoken because I cannot never speak at all, I fall into the contingency of language.

Parain insists that individual consciousness is animated by its subjection to the movement of language and is thereby made only to follow the universal movement of consciousnesses. If, on the contrary, it were absolutely autonomous, revolt would be pushed to the extreme and would be imprisoned in silence, as is the case with Kierkegaard's "demonism" described in *The Concept of Anxiety*.[7] What's more, an autonomous consciousness would suppose a world that is itself immobile, a world where it would have no efficacy [*elle ne serait pour rien*]. In fact, it forms with language a whole of which it is only the isolated part, affecting the other parts of actually possible becoming by receiving a body. Through its association with language, our consciousness, in relation to the movement of other individual consciousnesses, finds itself in the situation of a writer who can no longer recall the historical meaning of his work. It does not belong to him because he himself belongs to others from the moment that he writes. *Through language we are always outside ourselves. Our outside is the domain of language, which is exterior to us, but from which we cannot escape.*[8]

The solution suggested by Kantian idealism is no longer to judge but to describe. Life creates values, resolves all contradictions. It joins us to experience. Identical to God, we make everything happen through our consciousness, which grasps the world. Without it, it collapses. We are a beginning; we ourselves are the ground of our absolute freedom. Then why does this consciousness still need experience in order to know itself and *need to be described in order to say at the end of it all that it exists for nothing and that it suffers?* Parain remarks that, in truth, consciousness is immortal because it is already dead. It is immortal because it resides in the immortality of language, maintained by the infinite whole of individual consciousnesses that succeed one another under its law. And it is a play on words [*c'est jouer sur les mots*] to call this whole *Dasein* (being-there).

Having only a moment of imaginary existence, individual consciousness is immediately lost in the name that it is given. Coupled to language, *its function is to lose itself in it since only language appears.* Incapable of being contemplated without its intermediary, either it is not being but only feeling, or it is only the name that it gives to this feeling, thereby transmitting itself to language; the infinity that is then born is that of speech.

The truth is that "consciousness is there not to question, but to respond, since it is language that questions and consciousness is in the position of the accused."⁹ In and for itself, consciousness would not speak. From the moment that it speaks, it is for another. But this is not at all how the other is apprehended. The other is knowable only under the form of language, *because the other itself is language*. Language is thus the stranger inside us. "We are the stranger," says Parain. "There is no subject except an unstable subject of which only the name of the subject, which is already the object, appears. Such is our condition. This is why I call it a condition of revolt and generalized suicide."¹⁰

Nevertheless, Parain does not want to reduce consciousness to moments of anxiety and revolt and he sees its true reason for being in its refusal of any solution that avoids the metaphysical problem of its origin. If speech makes us responsible for history, guilty for speaking, we are capable of truth only through language; it is not only a source of our culpability, it is also our salvation. If it ruins the individual consciousness's dream of autonomy, it preserves the body for the common consciousness: it saves us from the suicide to which our revolt carries us by the promise of a universal meaning that recoups every cry of distress. Luther said: Whoever cries out, obtains grace. And if this has a universal meaning, then this meaning supposes an equality that grounds a new freedom.

How is this equality constituted?

We must accept our duplicity as a necessary law; not that it is a question here of *two states of language* which would be our immediate expression judged by an "immobile" consciousness, both author and spectator. It is a question of a dialogue that is pursued in each of us and from others to us, in an indirect expression of ourselves: *I can never say what I lack and there is always a margin of absence between my words and myself that comes to fulfill my acts, my death, and that of others*.¹¹ This is what Parain calls a *nostalgic rapport* with language that makes us a *deceptive appearance* for others. Because language is necessarily incarnated in order to lose its irresolute freedom, *it is not satisfied with its body any more than its body is satisfied with it and sooner or later we will disappear in the adopted language*, a language that, placing us *outside of ourselves* as well as outside of others, thus *prevents us from judging ourselves and from judging anyone else*.¹² Through this experience to which it submits each of us, language establishes an equality between us, an equality that is nothing other than that before death. Because we are not united and complete beings, but open and incomplete, death is introduced into our body by language in order thereby to obtain our unity and completion. The other aspect of our equality now appears: equality before the Logos, thus before God. In effect, because the very meaning of equality (which ought to assure us of our participation in truth) requires *a single judge who cannot be one of us*, there is a possible equality only before him.¹³ By this fact, we are temporally free in relation to each other to obey the rule of our carnal existence, which is to utter the speech of our own death. "It is not in dying at the hands of men," says Parain, "that one recognizes there is nothing more to say. Every premature death *is a new begin-ning*."[14] Here again, Parain provides a commentary on Blanchot's theme of the *impossibility of dying.*

Sartre, citing a passage from *Retour à la France* [*Return to France*][vi] where Parain claims that there is no better proof for the existence of God than the impossibility of man doing without language or directing it, goes on to note that Parain does not formulate this proof. But, in his *L'Embarras du Choix* [*The Trouble with Choice*], Parain states that, if it is not in our power (accord-ing to Leibniz) to first prove the possibility of this existence, the transcen-dence of language (because language is our possible) reestablishes the onto-logical argument.[15] The presence of names that language imposes on us makes the ideas that they represent dependent upon human thought. And if men can question these ideas, they still cannot undermine what these names des-ignate, nor even undermine these names. "Man can deny God only in words, thereby reaffirming him, his capability, because it is given by language, remains that he cannot destroy even by destroying himself."[16] Parain observes that it would thus be contradictory for the existence of God (otherwise called existence) to depend on human thought—as though existence could depend on those whom it made exist, because they do or do not think of it. "If we know only phenomena, then we must abolish the verb to be from our lan-guage." Every name of existence—the most ordinary as well as the most noble—asks to be.[17] If Sartre then declares that Parain would not dare to pro-pose that God maintains the identity of the word [*du mot*] in us, because then "it is God who thinks in us and we fade away; God alone remains,"[18] Parain will necessarily respond affirmatively. Language, whose meaning must be found, is imposed on us unilaterally, and this is even more true of "the most noble name of existence." However, *it is precisely our death that allows names to be* because language does not belong to us individually and will find another body after ours disappears. According to Parain, to form a noncontradictory idea of God is our ultimate task, and for him this coincides with the search for a just language. This search acquires an eschatological meaning for Parain. Because language never appears in its totality, it develops only through the death of individuals, and this is why peace on earth seems impossible. In the face of the impossibility of this peace, which is only the impossibility of ever attaining to this *just language*—because it is impossible ever to exhaust the possible—Parain conceives conversely of a *just silence*, more just than any language could humanly be; the just language being nothing other than God himself, the just silence would on the contrary consist and be born from our acceptance of responding *at each moment with every word.*

---

vi. Brice Parain, *Retour à la France* (Paris: Grasset, 1936), p. 16.

It is clear from then on why the problem of language is central for Parain: *because truth is revealed by language, only language allows us to find truth again; there is no truth to discover outside of this revelation.* Parain's thought thus completely coincides with the dogma of which it is ultimately only a demonstration: language has created man, it has revealed man to himself; without language there is no self-consciousness at all. Without language, nothing remains for man except the paths of experience. In subordinating experience to language, man founds logic. In subordinating language to experience, the former becomes prey to dialectic; however, death puts an end to it and language always subsists.

For Parain, our modern dialectic is only an aspect of the eternal dialogue of language and the flesh in which the Logos has spoken the first word and has also reserved the last; such is the true ground of what Parain understands by *logic*, which he does not confuse with formal logic. In his "Critique of the Materialist Dialectic,"[19] Parain describes the persistence of the Logos through the insoluble situations and contradictions that we live and express—whether in Hegel's dialectic of propositions, Marx's dialectic of experience, or in the dialectic of art. We believe that these dilemmas and situations are resolved, but these resolutions never do anything but reproduce our failure before a world that we did not create but for which we are nevertheless responsible because we speak.

Communism is only one stage of the grand historical revolution begun with the Reformation through the substitution of dialectic, a doctrine of experience, for the logic grounded on Revelation.[vii]

The paradox is that communism has contributed to reestablishing the *reign of the idea over the individual,* which amounts "to reconstituting the preliminary and necessary condition for the birth of a new idea of God."[20]

Communism is first founded upon the inversion of an essentially religious idea: equality before death and before God. The inversion of the idea provoked by the experience of material inequality as given primarily by the human condition justified its "second, scientific foundation": dialectical materialism and its political, economic, and social applications.

Hegel preserved only the triumph of language over existence, abandoning existence "to its fate as victim." It is here that Marx interrupts with his reproach that everything in this system is turned on its head, and [announces] his intention to put things back on their feet. In doing this, giving everything to the body, to the flesh, he neglects the soul, and, according to Parain, language. If the spiritual commerce of men were simply a direct emanation of their material behavior, one would be faced with a useless monologue, a cry

---

vii. *L'Embarras du Choix,* p. 134.

in the desert. However, our law is indeed the dialectic, Parain says, but what restrains it is the dialogue between the flesh and language, "the body calling for its contrary in order to be what it is not and language coming to its aid."[21] According to him, Marx has only applied to work the propositional dialectic that Hegel applied to consciousness.

Parain reproaches *Hegel for having stopped at the birth of the dialectic of language and existence; if he had pushed this dialectic further, he would have ended up by questioning its rights to experience,* let us say to the *freedom of experience.*[22] With its taste for freedom, experience tends to forget that it created neither language nor the world. But death returns to insinuate itself into it just when it is going to give up its attempts *because it is never finished with them.* Having never rested, how can it take the time to write? This inconsistency is all the greater precisely because writing—and here Parain joins Blanchot again—*to write is to kill what is movement and life.* "*With its mania for experience,*" Parain rightly says, "*humanity has effectively ceased to be able to look its mortal condition in the face. This is the secret of our modern despair.*"[23]

In order for experience to bear witness to our power of truth, which can hold us breathless until it is satisfied, it must have at its disposal not only the immortality of the soul but also that of the flesh. This objection by Parain returns us to the last judgment before which no speech could be totally decisive. Experience can be taken as a proper object of description only when death, the source of its fundamental uncertainty, is rejected. The dialectic of both Marx and Hegel supposes that science exhausts all of our cares. *It forgets that the individual wants to know why he disappears prior to being able to end his experience.*[24] Science thus never eludes the image of death that art represents because there is contradiction other than that discovered by the dialectic, a contradiction that is "the law of our tragic union with language": revolt is in the world.[25]

If science only gives an account of error, then art gives an account of falsehood because it indicates the more fundamental contradictions between what we are and the expression of a situation that, precisely in expressing it, we are incapable of taking on.

Parain sees here the source of the two solutions proposed to our generation: aesthetic (Kierkegaard and Nietzsche), and scientific (Hegel and Marx). "The aesthetic solution is grounded on the indifference that one acquires in cultivating art."[26] If I devote myself to language, this is because I cease to love myself after having preferred myself to others. But my flesh is what loves and I can no longer love when I am at the point of losing it. This law holds for both civilizations and individuals. A civilization uses its body, and always seeks other bodies to incarnate its soul. When this soul abandons it through an error of the flesh incarnating it, the individuals suffer this dissociation intimately. It is then that, pushed by the need to free myself from a dead atmosphere, I am withdrawn from life. Parain sees in the dialectic of art "a kind of differential calculus" that would allow for the calculation of the collective decline of a civilization through individual drama. In this universal dissociation, the aesthetic solution would be my own because it offers me the chance of uttering the speech before death that "will provide me my place," the meaning that I have in history. But if art transforms "emotion into just [*juste*] language," it only does so through indifference, "a sacrifice of the flesh" that produces the image of death. Emotion is so irrefutable that from the moment it is translated into words death, "valuable or useless," reverts entirely to a question of truth or falsehood. If the words of art express a cry, this is because they are not taken up by discussion but by power—we would say the authority of emotion—and Kierkegaard's profound objection to Hegel, according to Parain, is that the dialectic of propositions is explaining rather than *responding* to the cry and healing it.

Ultimately, because Parain's thought is completely centered on the flesh, its loss and its resurrection, it poses the following question: because it is experimental, does the materialist dialectic provide the response to the dissociation of flesh and language, and would it satisfy the plaint of the cry expressed in the dialectic of art?

If every civilization uses the body in which it is incarnated and if the idea that it represents is always in search of other bodies where it could survive, then the materialist dialectic ought to prove its truth by at least preventing the death of a civilization, since it is true that it still knows nothing contrary to the death of the individual, let alone anything of the cry that is expressed by art. From this again emerges the fact that the meaning of art would be to extend the dialogue between existence and language beyond the dialectic of propositions, beyond science, because experience is never finished until it has abolished the image of death; art always signifies the ruin of experience. Thus is revealed a fundamental dialectic of which that of propositions and that of science would be only stages, the dialectic that goes from silence to silence: "I am born in silence and I die speaking so that the silence of my death can speak." Art expresses this dialectic in this way: believing that it comes from my emotion, that is to say from *nothing*, my speech wants to return to this nothing. (This is an important aspect of Maurice Blanchot's thought.) On the contrary, religion pronounces: if my speech, coming from language (here Parain means God), lends itself to emotion in order to express it, then my speech returns to the language that is God.

Thus for Parain the primacy of language over experience is revealed by the *incapacity of our intelligence "to recuperate a body"* [*se refaire un corps*] and in the questioning of our experimental knowledge, it feels like a malediction that "always obligates us to persevere without having a beginning."[27] And it is only when suffering or death threatens to impose silence on us that we are even more concerned with taking on language.

It is this dialogue of language and existence, this dialogue of flesh and language marked by art that, in the assessment of civilizations as of the life of individuals, shows that "falsehood is paid not only in silver but by death." Notably, in the domain of work, I assume an order where I give a living part of myself to myself; this order comes to me from language which gives a meaning to the silence of my devotion and a speech on behalf of my already-spent energy. Thus I always speak of what I cannot accomplish, such that *what I say*, being *true* for *others*, is nothing but *falsehood* for myself at the moment when death comes to take me.

Observing this reversal of roles in the events of history, Parain already outlines here the negative aspect of the communist enterprise, expressed by propaganda, while its positive aspect is constituted only by the silence of those who are sacrificed through its effort.

Because the dialectical solution always requires "that one undertake what is most necessary . . . the least foreseen, with sacrificial rather than with economic means, against oneself and not for oneself,"[28] the communist revolution is not produced, as Marx foresaw it, in Germany where the industrial conditions offered favorable terrain for a scientific revolution, but in Russia, amid the absence of any industrialization and, because of this absence, by way of an antagonism between material needs and the needs of art, between *life* and *death*: on one side, the hope of dividing the lands according to the farmers and their belief in the resurrection of the flesh, and on the other side the nihilist tendency of the *intelligentzia*. The scientific and experimental dialectic reestablishes the law of dialogue between language and flesh at the very moment of its application. It thus creates a religious situation in spite of itself.

At the same time the fundamental deficiency of the materialist dialectic becomes manifest: "it does not give an account of the role of *existence in history*"[29]—which is the condition of the individual led to interpret the situation that it makes for him. If everything that happens can only ever lead to freedom, I will have prepared myself to die, that is to say that I will have sacrificed myself to language. By rendering me responsible for universal destiny, communism still subordinates me to language and thus to an act of faith. Only *this act of faith permits the individual to plug the gaping hole that the experiential formulas allow to remain.*[30]

Out of this situation, Parain will distinguish the path that returns to logic through the dialectic. As the dialogue between the flesh and language alone prevails—because of the practical application of science to human life—the reactions of men and events, insofar as they are products in the course of the Soviet experience, themselves testify to the necessary relation between the flesh and the Logos.

Ultimately the use of an experience supposes a double interpretation of the possible: either I evaluate the possible solely upon the condition of attempting its realization through the sacrifice of my own flesh or that of others, confident in final success, and this remains an act of faith in the resurrection, or, on the contrary, I seek an evaluation of the price of the realization of the possible and I would reject any experience according to the recognition of a law that restrains me from attempting and in some way *saves me from the very temptation of the experimental possible*; it is then that from the dialectic that employs the body, I return to the logic that recuperates it.

Just as "Russia's religious instinct" prevails "over its taste in art," one must recognize the return of the lesson of experience under the sign of logic. This is the case when Lenin declares, on the day following the seizure of power: "And now we must work"; it is the case much later when Stalin abol-ishes the rule of a revenue ceiling for Party members, instituting instead an inequality of salaries corresponding to an inequality of yields. For Parain, the norm that is thus established over individuals is the same, "if one considers it well, as that of *Genesis*: 'You will earn your bread by the sweat of your brow.'"[31]

The antagonism between the East and the West thus seems to come from two different interpretations of experience and freedom, from a false idea of the nineteenth century: *the idea that we know only through experience*. In the West this false idea draws its notion from freedom and its aesthetic. Precisely through its concrete application by Russia this false idea has returned, according to Parain, to the discipline of logic that has kept it free of an aes-thetic notion of freedom. Communism certainly is not and could not be a regime of freedom because it is, despite its propaganda, the connection of all in silence. In the current phase of its inequality of conditions, it establishes an equality of all in "the common incapacity to easily speak the truth, and consequently in the constant danger of lying, that is to say that of the longest discretion before decisive speech."[32]

This is just as well because, for Parain, communism would "only make sense if it persisted as long as necessary in silence and submission, so that the word to say appears at its hour, with the greatest expectation and as a sole sovereign."[33] Only in this way is Parain opposed to the aesthetic idea of free-dom in the West, an idea that arises from philosophical idealism and that continues to be expressed by phenomenology and modern existentialism; finally, in the nihilistic tendencies of literature, first there is a reaction to his-torical and social realities, and then to experimental knowledge, before which it in turn forms the notion of a necessarily aesthetic experience. Thus Nietzsche and all of modern paganism in his wake recreate the myths that they want to destroy. Our Western humanism ends in a generalization of the idea of art for art's sake and consequently in a culture of the powers of death. Because after having abandoned logic—the reign of the Logos speaking in the flesh—for the doctrine of experience, the West still has not become con-scious of the dialogue between flesh and language—it has produced for us a rupture of equilibrium at the expense of the powers of life and fecundity, and in favor of the powers of death represented by art and by a dissociation of existence and language.

Brice Parain's thought has not stopped evolving since *L'Embarras du Choix*. As soon as—and to the extent that—his predictions are confirmed, that events conform to the predictions, the reference to Soviet Russia will acquire its purely spiritual signification. Was there ever any other? For Parain, none of the social systems competing today, whose notions crudely deform the most grievous mortal questions, can furnish an authentic response to the single authentic questioning: interior questioning. And the resulting quarrels are only so much empty air [*vent*]. The *place of silence* created in Russia is not the result of a free decision. It could happen in the West, particularly in France, provided that it is a question of a free submission to the law of the dialogue between flesh and language. But the very principle of this law, of this exchange, resides in the belief that a truth exists. This primordial condition is lacking, however, in a teaching in which the principal point of departure, Parain notes, is the absence of truth. And without the belief in a true teaching, nothing is possible. To put it differently: experience remains stripped of meaning if it does not imply the knowledge of error. What Parain wants us to learn to retain is the lesson of an experience whose quality, although it was of tragically false inspiration, is such that, like all rigorously practical experience, it leads to human nothingness, to a point of intersection of human speech and grace. The teaching that we ought to draw from it is that, whatever speech we may say, it must respect us in our flesh, if it is a speech of sacrilege and perdition: our flesh will soon have exhausted the temptations of experience; it cannot escape the condemnation of our language, and as soon as our flesh can no longer either serve or subjugate it, we will find ourselves subjugated to *our immortal speech*. When man is completely exhausted or can no longer do anything to find a reason that sustains his life, speech remains, either for him to say to himself, or for someone to say who is not equal to man but beneath and outside of him, if not also as close to him as the speech of confession; to repeat his exhaustion, his failure, is to postpone [*differer*] his suicide; on the contrary, to address oneself to someone who understands and who understands even better because he has anticipated failure, is *to pray*. (*The great advantage of the one who believes in God is that he can be silent when there is nothing to say, because he knows that God takes care of things when necessary . . . the only attitude conforming to the scientific spirit.*) In prayer man testifies to truth about his error: he takes truth as a witness of what he endures, but *without having any right to life*. He obtains the grace to make a new beginning. Yet he cannot remake this new beginning, this new life; he can only be put in the position of taking this life as a *gift*, a being that does not rightfully belong to him but which befalls him by grace.

Chapter Seven

On Maurice Blanchot[i]

═══════════════════════

Contrary to a purely symbolic interpretation of the dogma of the resurrection of the flesh, Tertullian presents it in these terms: "If representation resides in the image of truth, and the image itself in the truth of being, the thing must exist for itself before serving as image for another. Similitude is not grounded in the void, nor parable upon nothingness."[1] All of the consequences that Parain draws from his conception of language are already present in these propositions. If Tertullian's proposition is then inverted, one would have circumscribed the sphere in which Maurice Blanchot's meditation moves. If representation resides in the image of truth, truth is only ever an image and the image is itself only an absence of being, thus a presence of nothingness; this is even what language itself consists of: for in order for a thing to be able to serve as the image of another, it must cease to exist for itself. An image of a thing designates nothing but the absence of this other thing. And in this way not only does nothingness ground similitude, it is similitude itself. Similitude of what? Is it not of a being that is dissimulated?

According to Maurice Blanchot, this notion of the dissimulation of being in language reveals the function that language exercises in the existent, which is that of death. But even this function of death is double. "Death is both the work of truth in the world, and the perpetuity of that which supports neither beginning nor end."[2] The ambiguity of language proceeds from this duplicity of death.

The existent seems to be composed only of the search for a meaning; it is nothing other than the possibility of a beginning and an end. Signification in existence proceeds from its very finitude, namely, the movement toward death.

Language, inasmuch as it signifies, can only do so in its reference to insignificance. What is this absence of signification? Being as being, because it is without beginning or end.

---

i. We have retained only the final part of a study on Maurice Blanchot published almost fourteen years ago in *Les Temps Modernes* (February 1949). This note perhaps can make up for the lacunae of our previous interpretation and rectify its perspective.

85

If death did not put an end to beings, if every thing had always to exist, there would be no more language, and thus no signification; every existent would immediately collapse into the absurd, namely, into being.

But death itself throws into the insignificance of being without beginning or end that which, in the existent, namely, in this world, acquires a meaning that survives it in the world and in history, but that it "absurdly" survives in being. This is why language draws its signifying force from the presence of nothingness in beings; it is "this life that carries death and is maintained in it."[3]

The insignificance of being without end renders signification inseparable from dying. But meaning, if it is possible only from a beginning and with an end in view, is not meaning if it does not remain in the existent by becoming endless retraction insofar as a world is this context of vicissitudes that one calls history.[4] Thus meaning rests upon the being that consecrates the impossibility of an indifferent meaning. But here is what is properly unbearable for the world: the existent as world is formed from the powerlessness of ever thinking being as being.[ii]

Between the meaning of existents and the being forever where sense is lost [s'abime], is situated that region called Literature, or Art. The work acquires a meaning outside of existence, which makes it a participant in being, which is deprived of meaning. And the search for a beginning, that consists of the existence of a creator who perpetually rejects his existence in word and image, bears witness to the insufficiency of signification in relation to being; the more signification the work attains, the more the creator tends toward the insignificance of being.

If the existent—the world and its history—recovers from forgetting being as insignificance—nevertheless, in the existent, speech and image, which have become signifiers, "sub-come" to ["sous-vient" à][5] insignificance, but there it is still the Remembrance [Souvenir] of what in itself is only an absence of all memory, therefore forgetting: being, this perpetuity that supports neither beginning nor end.

In the same way that the existent avoids the remembrance of being as being in its apprehension of an absolute insignificance, names prevent the forgetting of being in finite beings. Names are then already, in the same way as the image, a presence of nothingness in existents, and nevertheless, to signify them as such, they constitute them in being and restore them as insignificants [et les restituent insignifiants]. As constituted in being, death makes them survive in their meaning, being for ever, since always [étant à jamais, depuis toujours]. But constituted in being, from the beginning they have lost their identity, only signifying in the finitude of the existent. Identical in their temporal signification, but dissimilar to themselves, there where they are forever lacking meaning—in being without beginning or end.

---

ii. Heidegger observes (in *Nietzsche*) that metaphysics has never been able to think being except under the mode of the existent. But if the existent is inconceivable without being, it is no less in a perpetual dereliction in relation to the being that it deserts, and from which it endlessly absents itself [s'absentant]: this is the origin of all metaphysics.

Thus the names of existents, like images—metaphor, as well as the portrait (the images [imagines] or ancestral busts of Roman antiquity)—anticipate this dissemblance of existents in relation to their identity, in the being beyond death; while on this side of death they express the presence of nothingness in beings, namely, their absence: to the degree that their names throw the existents back outside of themselves.

In the communication between beings the portion of being's insignificance in each one interferes with the signification that they are given, namely, the mutual acceptance of their disappearance.

But then the relation with the dead [les disparus] intervenes, and in it the signification of a name, in which the dead one [le disparu] survives, is again made ambiguous; it is no longer the same in relation to its nonexistent self, because it is irrevocable, nothing but a past identity that remains in the existent mourning, memory, worship; in other words the last mask of what hides the indifference of what since its disappearance no longer has, but has never had, either beginning or end—is it the same again that signifies this or that for us? And when it signifies it, is there not in our relations this insignificance in ourselves that prevails over all, as long as two beings are able to attribute to each other what in them has never had beginning or end and which the one rejects in the other as perpetually deferring the being that they are unable to communicate, but that befalls them and reunites them in insignificance?

Without a doubt this is the secret of the incommunicable, which strikes [frappe] a vision from silence. Whoever sees in this way, must express himself in order not to alienate the world, and he describes what he sees in order to combat his alienation, although he only speaks to himself and can only be heard by the vision that comprehends him, such that his language is the speech of what is silent.[iii]

---

iii. "The man who speaks works [exerce] at once the negation of the existent of which he speaks and of his own existence, and this negation is worked by his power of being removed from himself, of being other than his being. Moreover: speech is not only the nonexistence of the thing spoken; speech as nonexistence becomes objective reality." Cf. *Literature and the Right to Death*, in *Critique*, XX, January 1948 ["Literature and the Right to Death," p. 324].

Death Sentence [English translation by Lydia Davis (Barrytown, NY: Station Hill, 1998)], through its texture and elements, still belongs to visionary literature, as long as its theme is the communication of a dead being with other dead beings; but it departs from it as long as this communication is established in the death of beings "from speech" in a meaning where speech "is this life that carries death and that maintains itself in it" (loc. cit.). Thus the power of putting beings to death, which speech exercises, must enter on the same level in death as a place of communication of beings, not only of communication, but of union. But, because death both constitutes the meaning of man and abolishes this meaning by abolishing itself, delivering the man who has ceased to be a man, beyond death, to the existence henceforth deprived of signification, this possibility presupposes death less than dying itself, namely the impossibility of dying, a dead time [une fois mort], the experience of dying without end, as a source of perpetual temporalization. Thus the concrete experience that offers the most perfect image of this temporalization is the case of the

But what has the same denomination of being as being, if it is equivalent to insignificance in the absence of a beginning and an end?

The language signifying the existent gives to absolute insignificance the "the most noble name of existence," namely, God.

The relationship thus established between this name, supreme among names, and the totality of the existent—if it is not simply a designation of language by

---

incurable sickness, in which the medical sentence: *As you ought to be dead in two years, the rest of your life is excessive*, constitutes the dying subject. An example that is nevertheless only a quite particular analogy with the Speech of Beginning: *the day when you will eat of it, you will certainly die.* Ultimately, the law that condemns to death the man originally destined to life, makes of him not a dead one [*un mort*] but a mortal. Death will come to him in the same way as immortality, as a modality of his being without which he would give up substance, from then on suspended between death and immortality. If original sin consists in the choice of death, it appears as man attaining dying and the experience of dying as a modality of his irrevocable existence.

So in *Death Sentence*, the sickness, that can still be at the origin of this knowledge, will serve only as a pretext for the demonstration of a more profound phenomenon of Blanchot's thought. The description of a concrete case of incurable sickness and survival by the medical condemnation will be identified with what language has itself revealed to Blanchot: the life of being from its putting to death by speech.

Here we are presented with the rare success of a communication with others, of the communication of an Erlebnis that, reproduced as it is in the *récit*, brings the reader to confront this form of immediate transmission of events with the theoretical translation of them in the important essay *Literature and the Right to Death*. "When I say: *this woman*, the real death of this woman is announced and already present in my language. The power of language is able to detach her from herself, subtracting her from her existence and from her presence." [323] A possible destruction, implicit in language. But it is because this woman is really capable of dying, at each instant menaced by the death "linked and united to her by an essential bond" that language can accomplish this "ideal negation." [ibid.] The first part of the *récit* is devoted to agony, to death followed by a temporary return to life of an incurable young woman. In his meditation on language, Blanchot insists upon the two movements of speech. If the *Lazare veni foras* "has had to leave the obscure cadaverous reality of its original ground and in exchange has only been given spiritual life."—language nevertheless knows that something must be excluded by the "terrible force that makes beings come into the world and by which they are lit [*s'éclairent*]. [326] Whoever sees God dies. What gives life to speech dies in speech: speech is the life that bears death and maintains itself in it." [327] So in its profound concern literature does not remain in this first movement: it wants to recuperate what language has destroyed—to recuperate the thing said as well as the thing destroyed; it wants the Lazarus of the tomb, not the resurrected Lazarus. It is in this way that by the incantatory power of the word, it makes *things really present outside of themselves.* The theme of the second part of the *récit* is the description of the links of a present being outside of itself with other beings outside of themselves that it makes present by its contact. In the first, the incurable young woman, named J, is dead from the medical point of view just like the "speaking" of the *récit*; J herself has a vision of "speaking" as well as death (p. 17 [25]), though she does not know it. [J.'s "vision" causes her to repeat the phrase "a perfect rose" a number of times.—trans.] A decision is made for

itself as returned by being to language—*is made to submit to this name (personal and essential) the fate of a* signified *existent.*

From the fact that this name would signify what it can never signify, what it comes to designate is absolute insignificance, namely, being; it constitutes being as a unique existent for the totality of the existent. This is the signification of the existent menaced by a single existent worthy of absolute insignificance and, as an indirect consequence, being itself menaced by a signification; namely, this same name submitted to the necessity of a beginning and an end.

Such seems to be the lesson of the parable of the Most High.

However, the analysis of this singular book that we have given so far bears essentially upon the scholastic distinction between being and existence, of being and essence; *it remains a valuable interpretation only as long as Blanchot's meditation on language touches on the ancient torment of thought, in its powerlessness to think being as being.*

THE MOST HIGH

The book opens upon the life of a man, a municipal functionary who, outside of his hours at the office, divides his sickly life between the clinic and a convalescence composed of disengagement and ambiguous contacts with his

---

a risky [*aléatoire*] treatment of injections that ought to restore her, but in her case risks killing her. There is a parallel here between the disintegrating action of common remedies and that entirely spiritual one of the thought of "speaking." The medicine itself represents the world hostile to the spirit, a world where the decay of the flesh is accomplished—while "speaking" is subject to the death that gives speech, and that also exercises the constitutive force of the existence from death [*à partir de la mort*]. Thus it can, by its presence beside what is considered dead, bring her back to the life of speech; nevertheless it can only be the time of a journey, after which the forces of the world to which we belong reconstitutes the cadaver insofar as "speaking" still belongs to the world. The life of speech must coincide with the total destruction of what the named object carries in itself of the world, so that existence begins without end, so that being begins according to the life of language that carries death and maintains itself in it.

In the *récit* the transcription of living events implicates an order of truth that is necessarily different from the theoretical discussion of this truth implicit to the experience. In this sense the *récit* is richer, but it is also more obscure. We have here a contact with the mystery independent of our comprehension, because we belong to this mystery, and what in us belongs to it thus remains as ungraspable to our reason as the incommunicability of lived and related fact. Maurice Blanchot's art thus consists in putting a part of ourselves into relation with what it says. As soon as we read what he says to us, we do not understand it, we understand even less that we are already included in his sentence [*phrase*]. And this is not because we do not understand that we are led to push further forward, but because we are constantly in search of this part of ourselves alienated by the *récit* that we want to recuperate at any price. As readers we also want to regain what experience transcribes [*transcrite*] of facts, which takes our adherence, abolished, or a *real presence*, beyond its abolition.

neighbors, unless his fatigue forces him to fall back on his family, composed of his mother who has remarried and a sister. Upon the return of this charac-ter from a holiday that he has just taken with his family, an epidemic of an indeterminate illness breaks out in the quarters where the building he lives in is located. The illness takes on apocalyptic proportions: riots, fires, repres-sions, cruelties, acts of terror. But instead of leaving his building—now trans-formed into a sordid dispensary—the novel's hero remains, as though he too, suffering from the sickness, is mired in the decomposing atmosphere. This is the exterior action as it appears to the absentminded reader. Perhaps he will never escape from the bewitchment that it exercises all by itself; there is an even greater chance that he will not remember the first words of the book at all: *I wasn't alone, I was anybody* [*j'étais un homme quelconque*]. *How can you forget that phrase* [*formule*]?[6] Let us hold fast to these terms: anybody—a phrase—such is the sense that Blanchot makes of language as the simultane-ously transcendent and immanent agent of our human adventure, a language both associated with, and separated from, anyone whatsoever [*un homme quel-conque*]; and in this way it also struggles against forgetting, a struggle that makes a memory out of it, but a memory separated from its subject. If lan-guage remains associated with someone [*un homme*], it will constitute the proper meaning of this person in terms of an established signification and both will be exchanged for truth. But as long as language is separated from someone with whom it was associated for a moment—because language exhausts the meaning of a person in the movement that is pronounced through the story and which is that of truth—the person becomes fortuitous; or better he is only lying, the story being the truth; or better he is the truth, and it is the story that lies. But this interpretation moves away from the true meaning at the point of grasping it.

During the holiday spent with his family, the ordinary man whose name will be mentioned only once, later, appears linked to his sister (Louise) by a sort of pact that goes back to their childhood, but actually testifies to an infi-nitely more remote origin as soon as one is enlightened as to the character's true "condition." The scene with the tapestry, on pages 52 to 55,[7] acquires its full meaning on pages 247–249[8] where another meditation is recounted. Louise drags her brother into a cemetery (a word that is passed carefully over in silence so that only a vast agglomeration of *empty* houses appears, a first evocation of what we know better as the "Western Quarter") and there, at the bottom of a vault, she submits him to a rite, a ritual execution, whose incan-tatory speech: "As long as I live, you will live and death will live. As long as I breathe, you will breathe and justice will breathe. . . . And now, I've sworn it"[9] is a speech that the ordinary man [*l'homme quelconque*] already understood and we too have already *gleaned some part of it*. This is because we are in the pres-ence of a separated memory here—it remains to be seen what memory—sep-arated from its subject—it remains to be seen what subject. Then comes the scene of the flight and the sister's pursuit of the brother: "I have no idea what she read in my look. Her eyes became ashen, something snapped, and she slapped me—*a slap that crushed my mouth*."[iv] From this point on, the silence of others becomes the speech of the ordinary man and everything that the others say is the same as what he conceals. To such an extent that "the events are enclosed in the words so that [afin que] the words may be read in the events."[v] Thus is revealed little by little the secret of a hero who, from an intimate and familial plane—an *adopted* intimacy and family—we see in the second part of the book passing onto the plane of the collective calamity, of the epidemic, in the midst of a reign of terror whose impotent consciousness he will be [*il sera la conscience impuissante*]. Why doesn't he manage to leave the Western Quarters, doomed to devastation, murder, and fire?

Suddenly, in the course of a conversation, we learn the name of the ordinary man. Henri Sorge? Must we not utter this *name* in the language of the *Holy Empire* of Metaphysics and translate: *Heinrich Sorge?* That is: *die Sorge* as one hears it at the University of Freiburg? A *"cura," cura pura?* A pure care—which is camouflaged under the *name* of *Henri*. A pure care, this is existence: the *Dasein* of Henri. But is it a matter of Henri's existence? Not at all. Henri is then only an essence that has received existence, but then the "novel" would lose its interest and the title of the book would be unjustified. Consequently, it remains only an explication: Henri Sorge figures an existence *without being such, ein soseinloses Dasein*, and this is why he is none other than this one that we have said does not have an essence because his *essence is his existence.*[vi]

"Whoever sees God dies," writes Blanchot "in the traditional sense. What gives life to speech dies in speech: speech is the life of this death, it is the life that carries death and maintains itself in it."[10] Here this formula applies to God himself from the point of view of his *Ungrund*. God would know the condition that Blanchot makes for literature, God would know this: an *abyss* (*Ungrund*) that asks to speak, says *nothing* [*rien ne parle*], *nothing* (the *Ungrund*) finds its being in speech and the being of speech is *nothing*.

---

iv. Page 75 [72]. This scene finds its counterpart on page 223 [232–233] and in the final scene.

v. Tertullian [*On the Resurrection of the Flesh*, trans. Peter Holmes, *Ante-Nicene Christian Library: Vol XV. The Writings of Tertullian, Vol II* (Edinburgh: T & T Clark, 1870), ch. 20, "Figurative Senses Have Their Foundation in Literal Fact. Besides, the Allegorical Style Is by No Means the Only One Found in the Prophetic Scriptures, as Alleged by the Heretics." "The realities are involved in the words, just as the words are read in the realities."—trans.]

vi. "And this is why there are philosophers who say that God has no "quiddity" or essence, because his essence is nothing other than his existence." (St. Thomas Aquinas, *De ente et essentia*, Book VI.)

What's more [À *plus forte raison*], God *is deprived* of his *name*, or existence
is deprived of being such because it is separated from the name of God in the
state of *care*; under this *borrowed name*, *Sorge*, "employed by the civil state," he
is renounced [*se renie*] in the life of a man, composed of different degrees of
nausea by which his consciousness embraces the universe that he has created
and who is now ruined even more and to the extent that he himself returns
into the *Ungrund*; nothing is left to chance in this singular parable and it is
therefore not in vain that the one who was *raised in the East* lives in the populated quarters of "the West."[vii] In the same way the obscure tendency of language that is uttered through literature "wants to grasp the presence of things
before the world is, as well as what subsists when everything is effaced and the
numbness [*l'hébétude*] of what appears when there is nothing" and which by its
"concern for the reality of things, for their unknown, free and silent existence," makes of language "a material without contour, a content without
form, a capricious impersonal force that says *nothing*, reveals *nothing* and is content to proclaim, by its refusal to say anything, that it comes from and returns
to the night," just as the *notion* of the divinity does: a return of Speech to its
Ungrund of which the phenomenon revealed by literature, which renders
things and beings outside of the world, is only the reflection.[11] And just as the
myth of the survivor was invoked, either of a man who believes that he is alive
because he has forgotten his death, or of another who knows that he is dead
vainly struggling to die, so now the myth of *a creator who keeps watch over himself*, while he would be *dead* in his creation, projects onto God a divine consciousness empty of his hypostases. Here the double polarity in the Word is
affirmed again as a function of the nothingness that it calls into being, and as
language is joined with a man and then abandons the man, so the Word of
God leaves God and contests what he has uttered. To such an extent that in
The Most High when he is questioned on the one hand by the State and the
law, and on the other hand by a revolt organized under the form of an epidemic and social devastation (which are found to be only the complicity of the
revolt and the suspect with the law that they combat, while acts of violence
and repression are only the human complicity of the law with the human
movements that it suppresses), we understand that it is a question here of an
interpellation engendered by the dialectic inherent to the Word: the State
with its law and its prisons—from which men no longer want to leave because
they have never been any more free than prisoners,[viii] and where the sick are
assimilated with the criminals and "receive through the punishment of death
the very error that this punishment makes them atone for"—are even here

---

vii. In Blanchot's book, the Western road becomes the theater of "the decline of the
Occident."

viii. Sade is the most poignant illustration of this.

only the images of the signification that one has decided to give to existence and the world, images that are, however, ruined or inverted by the impossibility—even by virtue of the possible infinity of language—of maintaining a signification formed through the elimination of *everything that wills only for itself and never dies.* The presence of the State, just like the presence of God, disposes of a ubiquity that resides in the universal faculty of speaking, one of recognizing and pronouncing the law, but also one of transgressing it by virtue of the presence of the law. If God, because he no longer speaks, or is no longer named, or because he speaks through the mouth of his enemies, returns to the *Ungrund* (and from then on language seeks to destroy signified things in order to know their real presence), in the order of facts, the epidemic is able to follow the revolt and to suggest this revolt as a consequence. The incurable illness can no longer be deciphered in the punishment or in the crime as what it in fact is: the will to grasp what the usage of words has abolished in favor of visible signification without ceasing to conceal its object, because it is itself an impossibility of dying.[ix] This is why Sorge says to Bouxx: "Please understand, *everything that you get from me is, for you, only a lie—because I'm the truth.*"[12] *Dei Dialectus solecismus.*[13] No one knows this better than the one who, beneath the name "Henri Sorge," has a consciousness as infinite as its impotence: for its impotence belongs to its own impossibility of dying, to its eternity. He who is existence, perhaps he aspires in turn to this death that gives signification; would existence be capable of it by renouncing its *being such,* by dying as God? Although he would "die" in the hearts of men—so one would explicate Blanchot's vision—he would consequently survive in himself, he would appear to have forgotten his "death," or at least be refusing to "remember it." This is how his reaction before the very old tapestry, gnawed by worms, must be understood: "Ah—a false, perfidious image, vanished and indestructible. Ah—certainly something very old, criminally old. I wanted to shake it, tear it apart, and, feeling enveloped in a fog of moisture and earth, I was gripped by the obvious blindness of all these people, by the crazily unconscious movement that turned them into agents of a horrible and dead past *in order to lure me as well into the deadest and most horrible past.*"[14]

A loyal functionary of the State, Sorge's "consciousness" is not "sick" enough to meditate upon "certain reforms," and, when the machine is disrupted, he instead wants to play its game well. Sorge insinuates his resignation more than he gives it: all of this behavior is therefore exactly the same as that of the *Most High.* Here is Sorge, vegetating amid the general devastation and, again, he bears the same attitude as that of a creator before his devastated creature: the creature can only contemplate suffering, and the former's assumption

---

ix. The epidemic is here a perfect illustration of contemporary thought and its literary expressions.

is only a feint on his part; to put this in a cruelly straightforward way, it was only to liken it to Sorge—he has only one preoccupation, that of dissimulating and confounding *his essence with his existence*, and this is what one ought to call his *immobility*. But, if every voice is only his own voice, then his silence is penetrated by another silence whose implicit accusation is intolerable to him: "You didn't hear them, and that was the worst. . . . Whole populations . . . without having anything to say . . . were ready to slide into the enormous hole into which history stumbled. It was this silence that hit me like a powerful scream, and howling, choking, whispering, it drove the listener—who just once had agreed to listen—crazy. And this cry of distress was universal. I knew that those who wanted the death of the law were screaming like the others; and I knew that this petrified silence, through which some continued to express their confidence in an unshakeable regime, to the point of not noticing what was going on . . . which, for others, meant confusion when faced with the impossibility of knowing where justice ended and where terrorism began, where informing for the glory of the State won out, and where informing for its ruin did too—I knew that this tragic silence was still more fearsome than anyone could have believed, because it was *emanating from the silent cadaver of the law itself, refusing to say why it had entered the tomb and whether it had gone down there to break open or to accept the tomb.*"[x] Then being is unmasked. It is first unmasked by an unknown woman in the building. "Going out, I said hello to a woman and opened the door for her. She looked at me for a moment, shuddered, and then, pale, threw herself gravely at my feet, with a well-considered movement, her forehead pressed against the ground; then she got up nimbly and disappeared. After she left, I got worked up with enthusiasm. I wanted to do something extraordinary—*kill myself*, for example. Why? Out of joy, no doubt. But now this joy seemed unbelievable. I felt only bitterness. I was overwhelmed and frustrated."[15] In extreme sickness, adoration is momentarily made clear. But does this joy fail to last because existence, beneath the name of which it is henceforth deprived, is now stronger than its adorable essence? Is it always the case that if adoration provoked in being a movement of generosity—"kill myself," for example—this movement was an irritant to its immutability, although here it is implied that it was the expected gesture in this case. He is almost immediately recognized by the strange nurse Jeanne, charged with his care, who confesses and *proclaims it*: "Now, now, I know who you are, I have discovered it, I have to announce it. Now . . . 'Be careful,' I said. 'Now. . . .' And she sat up suddenly, raised her head and with a voice that penetrated the walls, that overwhelmed the city and the sky, with such a full but calm voice, so imperious she reduced me to *nothing*, she screamed, 'Yes, I see you, I hear you, and I know that the Most High exists. I can celebrate him,

---

x. Blanchot, *The Most High* (228–9/220).

love him. I turn toward him saying, 'Listen, Lord.'"ˣⁱ Paraphrasing the words of
Scripture, Sorge scolds her: "Couldn't you have kept that to yourself?" But
here the divine essence is supposed to hide from and refuse its name: "Why did
you speak? Get this: I don't assume the burden of your little secrets. I'm not
responsible for them. I don't know what you said. I forgot it immediately."¹⁶
And it is existence deprived of being, the *Ungrund*, that responds: "Your words
mean nothing. . . . Even if they referred to something that's true, they would
be worthless."¹⁷ However, from the moment that the creator is discovered, as
he is shown here, reduced to Sorge's repugnant state, it is not surprising to see
him engaged in a jealous scene with Jeanne because she pretends to live with
him alone, but also lives with the doctor Roste. Only hindered beneath this
jealousy, the jealousy of a creator for his creature passes unnoticed, and then,
at the precise moment when she says "two obscenities" to him: "Suddenly, it
was as if I'd been awakened, and a strange feeling went through me: a feeling
of splendor, a majestic and radiant drunkenness. It was as if the day's events
and words had found a place in their true region."ˣⁱⁱ Perhaps this was the last
fragment of divine essence appealed to by his name, before which it vanishes
[*s'évanouisse*] into existence deprived of being: "I'm anybody." Henceforth is it
still a question of truth or of a mystification? And if it were true that this was
a mystification, would this not then provide a single account of the truth that
it is not? "I'd still like to be able to change my words into jokes, because I feel
their weight. But now you have to believe me. What I'm going to say is true.
Take me at my word, tell me you'll believe me, swear to it.—Yes, I'll believe
you. She hesitated, made a violent effort, and then lowered her head with a
kind of laugh: *I know that you are the Unique, the Supreme One. Who could stay
standing before you?*"¹⁸

Once recognized, he thinks of only one thing: to flee. How can the one
who is existence flee existence? Perhaps it can by hiding in the *Ungrund*,
since language resides among men, devoid of meaning: the words of the nurse
who has seen her adoration rejected no longer seem blasphemous: "I'm not
blind, she said. . . . As soon as I approach, you step away. If I go away, you
don't notice it. You never look at me or hear me. You pay less attention to me
than to a rag. . . . Why did you come here? I could ask you for a long time.
Why, right now, are you here, near me? If it's to mock me, I'm not ashamed,
I take pride in it. If it's to reject me, I'm not hurt, I'm stronger. Because I don't
give a damn about you, either. I know who you are and I don't give a damn
about you . . . I'll lock you up like a dog. No one will know anything about
you, no one other than me will have seen you . . . I expect nothing from you.
I've asked for nothing. I've lived without being concerned about your life.

xi. Ibid. (231/221), Klossowski's emphasis.
xii. Ibid. (232/223).

You should know that I have never, ever implored or begged you. I have never said: come, come, come!"[xiii]

As words become absurd, carried by the movement that dissociates essence from existence as long as the anticipated event doesn't appear—the impossible "death of God"—so also attributes break off from their subjects, accidents from their substances: odors, colors, and sounds are separated from the beings and things from which they emanate in order to return to "an existence that determines its *indetermination*"—as if even the things and beings created by the Word have lost their *essence*, their being such, in order to return to the state prior to their proliferation through the silence of the one that utters them, just as Sorge throughout his confession never ceases describing them to us since the scene in the cemetery when, whispering the name of his sister, he felt this name dissolve in his mouth, becoming anonymous "and I said no more."[xiv] This scene of ritual execution that is completed by the *slap that crushed my mouth*[19] finds its counterpart in the final scene of the book. If Louise, who brought him back to her room on the Western road and helped him there during a blackout, appeared to him then as "a nurse," the nurse Jeanne now evokes "his sister" in the "isolation ward"[20] where she transfers the one that she alone has recognized and who currently seems preoccupied only with his own "safety": "I knew that, whatever happened, I had to keep still now."[21] With this "immobility that scandalizes men. I remembered that *nothing* could happen and I remembered that *I knew it*. . . . This thought was extraordinarily comforting, in one fell swoop it restored everything." And then, thanks to the suppression of the divine name by unchained speech, what happens? Sorge begins to sweep his room "since the floor tiles were covered with dust, dried mud, even straw."[22] Existence "makes a little pile of sweepings" before "collapsing onto the garbage," gradually invaded by anguish in the privation of his being. And we witness everything that constitutes the stages of ontological decomposition (signaled by the apprehension of the toad, a vision of debasement)[23] until the final moment when the "Most High," wasting away in its "Abyss,"[24] sees its creation sinking into the original cesspool out of which Speech [*la Parole*] has drawn it: "A compact and gaping pile—a hole . . . it was absolutely motionless, lying on the ground, it was there, I saw it, completely and not its image, as much from within as from without; I saw something flow, solidify, flow again, and nothing in it moved, its every movement was total numbness, these wrinkles, these excrescences, this surface of dried mud its crushed insides, this earthen heap its amorphous exterior; it didn't start anywhere, it didn't end anywhere, it didn't matter which side you caught it from, and once its form was half perceived it

xiii. Ibid. (238/228).
xiv. Ibid. (70/73).

flattened out and fell back into a mass from which eyes could never get free. . . . The pile took no notice of my presence. It let me approach, I came still closer, and it didn't move; I wasn't even a stranger to it, I slid up to it like no one had ever done before, and it didn't hide, it didn't turn away, didn't ask for anything, didn't take anything away. Suddenly—and this I saw—a fairly long appendage, which seemed to be demanding a separate existence, came up out of the lump; it thrust itself out and stayed there, stretching; the entire mass turned slowly with idiotic ease and without budging. I encountered two little transparent orbs, lying on top, rootless, smooth, oily, extremely smooth. They weren't looking at me; no hint or movement came from them and I myself saw them no more than if they had been my own eyes, and already I was very close to them, dangerously close—who had ever been that close?"[xv] A powerful image of the fall into the indeterminate as well as the rapid blossoming of *something* out of the indeterminate; it doesn't matter whether this *something* here is the human condition, the divine condition, or simply the very condition of language.

The final scene—a scene where the prophecy of the cemetery is fulfilled—then appears as a great metaphysical play on words. The nurse Jeanne behaves like a reversed Madeleine. If Madeleine finds the meaning of existence in the void of the tomb, Jeanne needs to see existence descend into the tomb in order to know meaning for herself. She says: "You're not just something one dreams about (You, that is to say existence); I've recognized you. Now I can say: he's come, he's lived near me, he's there, it's crazy, he's there." Which again amounts to saying: existence has come, existence existed before me, existence is there. What's crazy is that the *essence of existence is to be existence.* And then: "Alive, you've been alive for no one but me. . . . Couldn't you just die of it?" She cannot bear that existence should be existence. Thus she says: "Now it's time. Your life has only been for me, so I'm the one who has to take it from you." And then: "Nobody knows who you are, but I know, and I'm going to destroy you."[25] This can have no other meaning than Meister Eckhart's: "when I know who existence is, I lose existence." The revolver that Jeanne, kneeling, aims at the one who is existence is nothing more than a prop that here conforms to the air of fabulation. It cannot literally be a question of "deicide," nor, in an anagogical sense, can it be a question of suicide. If it is in death that existence recovers speech, this speech must still be that of the Author; of the Author of the author, or simply of the author.

We have had the naïvete to interpret *The Most High* in the *literal* sense. Language imposes on us the presence of the name of God; if this name must ultimately have a meaning, because "all names demand being, both the most common and the most noble," and "our death serves this," how is language

---

xv. Ibid. (247–248/237–238).

reversed here in the eclipse of the noblest name of existence? Because its power of negation, being worthy of the absolute existence that this name designates, never ceases until it itself becomes absolute existence. In this sense, language would be the Most-High at the very moment when it names the Most-Base.[xvi]

---

xvi. "The more the world is affirmed as the future and the broad daylight of truth, where everything will have value, bear meaning, where the whole will be achieved under the mastery of man and for his use, the more it seems that art must descend toward that point where nothing has meaning yet, the more it matters that art maintain the movement, the insecurity and the grief of that which escapes every grasp and all ends." [Maurice Blanchot, The Space of Literature, trans. Ann Smock (Lincoln: University of Nebraska, 1982), pp. 247/260, note.]

Chapter Eight

Nietzsche, Polytheism, and Parody[i]

Parody and polytheism in Nietzsche? At first sight, it is not at all clear what
relation exists between these two terms, nor what kind of concerns would lead
one to speak of them, nor what interest one might have in raising such a question. If for most people Nietzsche's name is inseparable from the utterance *God
is dead*, then it may seem surprising to speak of the religion of *many* gods with
regard to Nietzsche. After all, there are countless people today for whom Nietzsche's name signifies nothing more than this utterance—and they did not
need Nietzsche to know that all the gods are dead. It may also seem, perhaps,
that I am simply using Nietzsche to demonstrate the existence of many gods
and to legitimate polytheism; and, by playing on these words, I will not escape
the reproach, under the pretext of showing the meaning of parody in Nietzsche, of making a parody of myself and thus of parodying Nietzsche.

　If I must open myself to such confusion, I would nevertheless like to
make one thing clear: insofar as one is led to interpret the thought of a mind
[*esprit*] that one tries to comprehend and make comprehensible, there is no
one who leads his interpreter to parody him as much as Nietzsche. This is true
not only of those interpreters who are smitten with his thought, but also
those who try hard to refute him as a dangerous spirit. Nietzsche himself
urged one of his first interpreters—no one had yet spoken of him—to abandon all pathos, not to take sides in his favor, and to put up a sort of ironic
resistance when characterizing him.

　Here, then, we cannot avoid being the victim of a sort of ruse, nor can
we avoid falling into the trap inherent in Nietzsche's own experience and
thought. Unless we simply undertake the work of the historian, as Andler
did,[1] the moment we try to elucidate Nietzsche's thought, he is always made

---

i. Lecture at the College de Philosophie, 1957.

to say more than he says and less than he says. This is not—as is often the case with other thinkers—due to a simple lack of perspective or even because a determinate point of departure has been omitted. In assimilating Nietzsche, we make him say more than he says, while in rejecting or altering him, we make him say less than he says—for the simple reason that, properly speaking, with Nietzsche there is hardly either a point of departure or a precise terminus. Nietzsche's contemporaries and friends were able to follow an evolution from *The Birth of Tragedy* to *The Wanderer and His Shadow* and on to *The Gay Science*, and from *Zarathustra* to *The Twilight of the Idols*. But those of us who have at our disposal the youthful writings as well as the posthumous work, including *Ecce Homo*, have not only been able to follow the ramifications of Nietzsche's posterity, and to witness the accusations made against Nietzsche as a result of recent historical upheavals, but have also been able to discern something which, I think, is not without importance: Nietzsche, who was despite everything a professor of philology at Basel, and thus an academic with absolutely certain pedagogical ambitions, did not develop a philosophy. Instead, outside of the framework of the university, Nietzsche developed variations on a personal theme. Living a simple life marked by extreme suffering and convalescence, forced to sojourn with increasingly frequency at health resorts, while in the midst of the greatest intellectual isolation, Nietzsche was thereby abandoned, in the most auspicious manner, to listen to himself alone [*à sa seule audition*].

This academic, trained in the disciplines of science in order to teach and train others, found himself compelled to teach the *unteachable*. What is unteachable are those moments when existence, escaping from the delimitations that produce the notions of history and morality, as well as the practical behavior derived from them, is shown to be given back to itself with no other goal than that of returning to itself. All things then appear at once new and quite old; everything is possible and everything is immediately impossible, and there are only two courses open to consciousness: either to keep silent, or to speak; either to do nothing, or to act so as to imprint on one's everyday quotidian ambiance the character of existence given back to itself; either to lose itself in existence or to reproduce it.

Nietzsche had immediately attained this unteachable in his own solitude, through his own idiosyncrasies—that is, *by describing himself* as a convalescent who had suffered from the unresolved nihilism of his own era and who had resolved this nihilism, to the point where he was able to restore to the notion of *fatum* its full force. He had grasped the very ground of existence, lived as fortuitous—that is, he had grasped that aspect of existence which, through him, was fortuitously named Nietzsche. In this way, he had also grasped the necessity of accepting this fortuitous situation as his own destiny (in the sense he ascribes to this word), which amounts to a decision to affirm the existence of a universe that has no other end than that of being what it is.

Nietzsche recognized this apprehension of existence—which is nothing other than the apprehension of eternity—in the simulacra of art and religion, but he also saw that this mode of apprehension is perpetually *denied* by scientific activity, which explores existence through its tangible forms in order to construct a practicable and livable world. Nonetheless, Nietzsche felt a solidarity with both these attitudes toward existence: that of simulacra, as well as that of science, which declares *fiat veritas pereat vita.*[2]

And so he put simulacra into science and science into simulacra in such a way that the scientist can say: "Qualis artifex pereo!"[3]

Nietzsche was prey to an ineluctable revelation of existence that did not know how to express itself except through song and image. A struggle was being waged within him between the poet and the scholar, between the visionary and the moralist, each of which was trying to disqualify the role of the other. This struggle was provoked by a feeling of moral responsibility toward his contemporaries. The different tendencies, the different attitudes that were fighting over Nietzsche's consciousness would endure until a crucial event was produced; Nietzsche would be externalized in a character, a veritable *dramatis persona*: Zarathustra—a character who is not only the product of a fictive redoubling, but is in some way a challenge by Nietzsche the visionary to Nietzsche the professor and man of letters. The character of Zarathustra has a complex function: on the one hand, he is the Christ, as Nietzsche secretly and jealously understands him, but on the other hand, insofar as he is the Accuser of the traditional Christ, he is the one who prepares the way for the advent of Dionysus philosophos.

The years during which *Thus Spoke Zarathustra* was fashioned, and especially those that followed its birth, were for Nietzsche *a state of unparalleled distress*. *"One pays dearly for immortality: one has to die several times while still alive. There is something that I call the rancor of what is great: everything great—a work, a deed—is no sooner accomplished than it turns against the man who did it. By doing it, he has become weak; he no longer endures his deed, he can no longer face it. Something one was never permitted to will lies behind one, something in which the knot in the destiny of humanity is tied—and now one labors under it!—It almost crushes one."*[4]

Zarathustra, to be sure, was latent in the previous works, but what is important for Nietzsche's life is not only the creation and presence of the ineffable songs of the poem. What came to be determinant for Nietzsche's life was the more or less complete identification of Nietzsche with this physiognomy, which for him constituted a kind of promise, a resurrection, an ascension. In a certain sense, Zarathustra is the star of which Nietzsche himself is only the satellite. Even better, I would say that Nietzsche, after having paved the way for the triumph of Zarathustra, remains behind in a position sacrificed in the course of a victorious retreat. As he himself said, he would pay dearly for this creation. Zarathustra prefigures Nietzsche's own immortality—

that immortality by which one dies more than once while still alive. When Nietzsche managed to separate Zarathustra from himself, and was thereby able to encounter him as a superior but still inaccessible reality, then the world of appearances—which, according to the divine fable, was created in six days—disappeared along with the true world; for in six days the true world became a fable once again. Nietzsche casts a retrospective glance at this refabulation of the true world that disappears in six days, or six periods, which are the inverse of the six days of the world's creation. It is this refabulation that he traces out in an aphorism of *The Twilight of the Idols* entitled *"How the 'True World' Finally Became a Fable."*

Here is the passage:

"1. The true world—attainable for the sage, the pious, the virtuous man; he lives in it, *he is it.* (The oldest form of the idea . . . a circumlocution for the sentence, "I, Plato, *am* the truth.")

2. The true world—unattainable for now, but promised for the sage, the pious, the virtuous man, "for the sinner who repents." (Progress of the idea: it becomes more subtle, insidious, incomprehensible . . . it becomes Christian.)

3. The true world—unattainable, indemonstrable, unpromisable; but the very thought of it—a consolation, an obligation, as an imperative. (At bottom, the old sun, but seen through mist and skepticism. The idea has become elusive, pale, Nordic, Königsbergian.)

4. The true world—unattainable? At any rate, unattained. And being unattained, also *unknown.* Consequently, not consoling, redeeming, or obligating: how could something unknown obligate us? (Gray morning. The first yawn of reason. The cockcrow of positivism.)

5. The true world—an idea which is no longer good for anything, not even obligating—an idea that has become useless and superfluous—*consequently,* a refuted idea: let us abolish it! (Bright day . . . return of *bon sens* and gaiety: Plato's embarrassed blush; pandemonium of all free spirits.)

6. The true world—we have abolished. What world has remained? The apparent one perhaps? But no! *With the true world we have abolished the apparent one.* (Noon, moment of the shortest shadow, end of the longest error: *Incipit Zarathustra!*)"[5]

With the true world, we have abolished the apparent world. When the true world (the Platonic, Christian, spiritualist, idealist, transcendental world) that serves as the point of reference for the apparent world disappears, then the apparent world disappears as well. The apparent world cannot become the real world of scientific positivism: the world becomes a fable, the world as such is only a fable. "Fable" means something that is narrated, and that exists only in its narration. The world is something that is narrated, a narrated event, and hence an interpretation. Religion, art, science, and history are so many diverse interpretations of the world, or rather, so many variants of the fable.

Is this to say that we are dealing here with a universal illusionism? Not at all. The fable, I said, is an event that is narrated; it happens, or rather, it must make something happen, and in effect an action takes place and narrates itself; but if we are not content to listen and follow, if we seek to apprehend the narration in order to discern whether *behind the recitation* there is not *some moment* that differs from what we understand in the narration, then everything is interrupted—and once again, there is a true world and an apparent world. We have seen how the true world and the apparent world have become a fable, but this is not the first time. There is something in Nietzsche's text that warrants mention: *midday,* hour of the shortest shadow. After midday, everything begins again, including the ancient world, that is to say, the past interpretations. In antiquity, the hour of midday was an hour at once lucky and ill-fated [*faste et néfaste*], not only an hour in which all activity was suspended under the blinding light of the sun, but also an hour of forbidden visions, followed by delirium. After midday, the day declines into shadows; but through these shadows, we will be guided to profound midnight by Zarathustra, the master of the fable.

Fable, *fabula,* comes from the Latin verb *fari,* which means both "to predict" and "to rave" [*prédire et divaguer*], to predict fate and to rave; *fatum,* fate, is also the past participle of *fari.*

Thus when we say that the world has become fable, we are also saying that it is a *fatum;* one raves, but in raving one foretells and predicts fate. We emphasize these connotations here because of the role that fatality—the crucial notion of *fatum*—plays in Nietzsche's thought. The refabulation of the world also means that the world exits historical time in order to reenter the time of myth, that is, eternity. Or rather, it means that the vision of the world is an apprehension of eternity. Nietzsche saw that the mental conditions for such an "exit" [*sortie*] lay in the *forgetting* (of the historical situation) that was preliminary to the act of creating: in *forgetting,* humans sub-come to [*sous-vient à*] the past as their *future,* which takes the *figure of the past.*[6] It is in this way that the *past comes to* [*advient*] them in what they create; for what they believe they create in this way does not come to them from the present, but is only the pronunciation of a prior possibility in the momentary forgetting of the (historically determined) present.

Zarathustra's mission is to give a new meaning and a new will to men in a world that he is necessarily going to recreate. But since every created world risks losing its meaning and becoming fabulous and divine once again, and since it may be rejected and seem intolerable to men now that they have come to will *nothing* rather than something, Zarathustra must reveal to them *the* true way, which is not a straight path but a tortuous one:

"For here is all my creating and striving, that I create and carry together into one what is fragment and riddle and dreadful chance."[7]

Along with the true world, we have abolished the apparent world—along with the preoccupation with truth, we have liquidated the explanation of appearances. ("*'Explanation' is what we call it, but it is 'description' that distinguishes us from older stages of knowledge and science. Our descriptions are better—but we do not explain any more than our predecessors.*"⁸) All this is full of consequence, for if the thought of having abolished the apparent world along with the true world is not a simple quip, it gives an account of what was happening in Nietzsche himself. He had given notice to the world in which he still carried the name of "Nietzsche" (and if he continued to write under this name, it was *in order to save appearances*): everything has changed and nothing has changed. It is better to let those who act believe they are changing something. Does not Nietzsche say that these people are not, in fact, men of action, but rather contemplatives who put a price on things—and that men of action act only by virtue of this appreciation by the contemplatives?

But this suppression of the apparent world, with its reference to the true world, finds expression in a long process that can be followed only if we take into account the coexistence, within Nietzsche, of the scientist and the moralist—or more essentially, the psychologist and the visionary. Two different terminologies result from this, which, in their perpetual interference, form an inescapable web. In the end, the lucidity of the psychologist, the destroyer of images, will simply be put to work by the poet, and thus for the fable. In his attempt to scrutinize the lived experience of the poet—the sleepwalker of the day—the psychologist would discover regions in which he himself was dreaming out loud.

This analysis of the psychologist, before he was invaded by the dreams and visions he tried to avoid, allows us to see succinctly how, in the name of the rational principles of positivism, Nietzsche winds up ruining not only the rational concept of truth but also the concept of conscious thought, including the operations of the intellect, and how, on the other hand, this depreciation of conscious thought leads Nietzsche to question the validity of any communicability through language; and we can see more clearly how this analysis—which reduces rational thought to impulsive forces, but which attributes to these impulsive forces the quality of authentic existence—leads to a suppression of the limits between the *outside* and the *inside*, a suppression of the limits between existence *individuated here and now* and *existence returning to itself* within the person of the philosopher. What presides over this disintegration of concepts—for obviously something must subsist—is always the intensity of the mind which has been excited to a supreme degree of insomnia, a sustained perspicacity that drives to despair the demand for integrity, a perspicacity whose rigor goes so far as to want to be liberated from these functions of thought as if from a final servitude, a final link with what Nietzsche called "the spirit of gravity."

The analysis of consciousness that Nietzsche gives in various aphorisms of *The Gay Science* may be summarized in the following observations:

1. Consciousness was the latest function to develop in the evolution of organic life; it is also the most fragile function, and consequently, the most

dangerous one. If humanity had become conscious all at once, as it has been believed, it would have perished a long time ago. The proof of this lies in the great number of false steps that consciousness has provoked in the life of the species, and that it continues to provoke in the lives of individuals, insofar as it creates a disequilibrium in their impulses.

2. This undesirable function (undesirable because it corresponds to an incompatible aspiration, the aspiration to truth) undergoes an initial adaptation to other impulsive forces; for a time, consciousness is linked to the life-conserving instinct, and then one forms the fallacious notion of a consciousness that is stable, eternal, immutable, and, consequently, free and responsible. Because of this overestimation of consciousness, its overhasty elaboration has been avoided. From this arises the notion of substance.

3. The mental operations that this (opportunely retarded) consciousness develops in its elaboration—these operations that constitute logical reason and rational knowledge—are merely the products of this compromise between the impulsive life and consciousness. From what is logic born? Obviously from the illogicality whose domain was originally immense. At this stage, according to Nietzsche's positivist description, logic becomes the strongest weapon of the impulses, particularly for those beings in which aggressiveness is translated into affirmation or negation, while illogicality remains the domain of the weakest impulses. Opportunely retarded in its own development, consciousness (as false consciousness) develops conscious thought out of the need to communicate through language. Such is the origin of the most subtle operations that constitute logical reason and rational knowledge.

"At bottom, every high degree of caution in making inferences and every skeptical tendency constitute a great danger for life. No living beings would have survived if the opposite tendency—to affirm rather than suspend judgment, to err and *make up* things rather than wait, to assent rather than negate, to pass judgment rather than be just—had not been bred to the point where it became extraordinarily strong."[9]

4. Consciousness, as a threatening function because of its antivital aspiration, therefore finds itself momentarily in retreat. In the relationship of knowledge, however, this dangerous power is manifested anew in its true light. Logical reason, constructed by the impulses in the course of this combat with the antivital tendency of consciousness, engenders habits of thinking which the still-maladapted tendency of consciousness is led to detect as errors. These *errors*—which are precisely those that make life possible, and which Nietzsche will later recognize as forms for the apprehension of existence—always observe the same rules of the game: namely, that there are durable things; that objects, materials, and bodies exist; that a thing is what it appears to be; that our will is free; that what is good for me is good in an intrinsic manner—ingrained propositions that have become the norms in accordance with which logical reason establishes the true and the nontrue.

"It was only very late," says Nietzsche, "that truth emerged—as the weakest form of knowledge. It seemed that one was unable to live with it: our organism was prepared for the opposite."[10] Hence, Nietzsche remarks, the strength of different sorts of knowledge does not reside in their degree of truth, but in their degree of antiquity, their degree of incorporation, their character as conditions for life. Nietzsche here cites the example of the Eleatics, who wanted to put our sensible perceptions in doubt. The Eleatics, he says, believed it was possible to *live* the antinomies of the natural errors. But in order both *to affirm the antinomy and to live it*, they invented the sage, a person who was both impersonal and unchangeable, and thus they fell into illusion (I am still citing Nietzsche). Unable to abstract from their own human condition, misunderstanding the nature of the knowing subject, and denying the violence of the impulses in knowledge, the Eleatics, in an absolute fashion, believed they could conceive of reason as a perfectly free activity. Probity and skepticism, those dangerous manifestations of consciousness, were able to develop in ever more subtle ways at the moment when these two contradictory propositions appeared to be applicable to life because both were compatible with fundamental errors—the moment it became possible to dispute about their greater or lesser degree of utility for life. Likewise, other new propositions, while not useful to life, were nonetheless not harmful to life because they were simply expressions in an intellectual game, and, consequently, they bore witness to the innocent and fortunate character of every game. At that moment, the act of knowing and the aspiration to the true were finally integrated as one need among other needs. Not only belief or conviction, but also examination, negation, mistrust, or contradiction constituted a power [*une puissance*], such that even the bad instincts were subordinated and placed in the service of knowledge, and acquired the prestige of what is licit, venerated, and useful— and ultimately the look and innocence of the Good. Nietzsche thereby comes to this first conclusion on the precise situation of the philosopher:

"*The thinker is now that being in whom the impulse to truth and those life-preserving errors clash for their first fight, after the impulse for truth has proved to be also a life-preserving power.*"[11]

The impulse to truth is a life-conserving power? But here this is only a hypothesis, a momentary concession. In fact, Nietzsche concludes with a question: "*To what extent can truth endure incorporation? That is the question; that is the experiment.*"[12]

Nietzsche himself will carry this experiment to its conclusion. When Nietzsche evoked the example of the Eleatics as an attempt to live the natural antinomies—an attempt that required the impossible impersonality of the philosopher in order to succeed—it was his own experience that he was projecting into the past. The Eleatics, said Nietzsche, invented the figure of the impersonal and immutable sage as being both One and All. In so doing, they fell into illusion, Nietzsche declares, because they remained unaware of the violence of the impulses in the *knowing subject*. But if Nietzsche, in this judgment against the Eleatics, presents himself as the person in whom this illusory experience has been brought to consciousness, it is precisely because he himself, obscurely, aspires to be both One and All, as if he now saw the secret of the experiment in *a return of consciousness to the unconscious, and of the unconscious to consciousness*—so completely and so well that, at the end as at the beginning, it would seem that the true world exists nowhere else than in the sage.

Here, we must immediately distinguish between the experiment to be performed and the lived experience [*l'expérience à faire et l'expérience vécue*], between *suffering* and *willing*.

In effect, we would like to know if the lived experience—Nietzsche's specific experience, the ecstasy of the eternal return in which the ego would suddenly find itself to be both one and all, one and multiple—could be made the object of a demonstration, and thus constitute the point of departure for a moral teaching.

But we must confine ourselves here to the question we posed earlier: Could the philosopher have knowledge of a state in which he would be both One and All, one and multiple, given the fact that he will always ascribe more and more consciousness to his pathos?

In other words: How could he possess his pathos knowingly insofar as the pathos would be an apprehension of existence returning upon itself?

In aphorism 333 of *The Gay Science*, Nietzsche provides a commentary on one of Spinoza's propositions that takes us to the heart of this problem:

The meaning of knowing.—*Non ridere, non lugere, neque detestari, sed intelligere!* says Spinoza as simply and sublimely as is his wont. Yet in the last analysis, what else is this *intelligere* than the form in which we come to feel the other three at once? One result of the different and mutually opposed impulses to laugh, lament, and curse? Before knowledge is possible, each of these impulses must first have presented its one-sided view of the thing or the event; after this comes the fight between these one-sided views, and occasionally these result in a mean, one grows calm, one finds all three sides right, and there is a kind of justice and a contract: for by virtue of justice and a contract all these instincts can maintain their existence and assert their rights against each other. Since only the last scenes of reconciliation and the final accounting at the end of this long process rise to our consciousness, we suppose that *intelligere* must be something conciliatory, just, and good—something that stands essentially opposed to the instincts, while it is actually nothing but *a certain behavior of the instincts toward one another*.

For the longest time, conscious thought was considered thought itself. Only now does the truth dawn on us that by far the greatest part of our spirit's activity remains unconscious and unfelt. But I suppose that these instincts which are here contending against one another understand very well how to make themselves felt by, and how to hurt, *one another*. This may well be the source of that sudden and violent exhaustion that afflicts all thinkers (it is the exhaustion on a battlefield). Indeed, there may be occasions of concealed *heroism* in our warring depths, but certainly nothing divine that eternally rests in itself, as Spinoza supposed. *Conscious* thinking, especially that of the philosopher, is the least vigorous and therefore also the relatively mildest and calmest form of thinking, and thus precisely philosophers are most apt to be led astray about the nature of knowledge.

In this very beautiful passage, I suspect that Nietzsche has defined, in a negative manner, his own mode of comprehending and knowing: *ridere, lugere, detestari* (laughing, crying, hating) are three ways of apprehending existence. But what is a science that laughs, or cries, or detests? A pathetic knowledge? Our pathos knows, but we are never able to share its mode of knowing. For Nietzsche, every intellectual act corresponds to variations of a state of humor. Now, to attribute a character of absolute value to pathos ruins, in a single blow, the notion that knowledge is impartial, since it was only from an acquired degree of impartiality that one called into doubt that same impartiality. This ingratitude is the inverse of knowledge, which is disavowed as soon as it makes us comprehend that we cannot know—an ingratitude that will give birth to a new impartiality, but within an absolute partiality. For if logical conclusions are nothing but the conflict among the impulses that can only end in something unjust, to aspire to more partiality would be to observe the highest justice.

If the thinker, as Nietzsche says, is the being in whom the impulse to truth and the life-preserving errors live and struggle together, and if the question is knowing to what extent truth can bear incorporation—if that is the experiment that must now be performed—then let us now try to see in what sense pathos is capable of this incorporation as an apprehension of existence. Now that the intellectual act has been devalorized—since it only takes place at the price of a supreme exhaustion—why not admit *hilarity* as much as seriousness as an organ of knowledge, for example, or anger as much as serenity? Once seriousness is admitted to be a state as doubtful as hatred or even love, why could not hilarity be as valid and obvious an apprehension of existence as seriousness?

The act of knowing, judging, or concluding is nothing but the result of a certain behavior of the impulses toward each other. Moreover, conscious thought—especially the thought of the philosopher—is most often the expression of a fall, a depression provoked by a terrible quarrel between two or three contradictory impulses that results in something unjust in itself. Does this mean that the philosopher (or the thinker or the sage, in the Nietzschean sense) should give himself over to a similarly contradictory behavior among the impulses? Or that he should never speak except in statements that participate in two or three simultaneous impulses, thereby giving an account of existence apprehended through these two or three impulses?

If the act of comprehending something is at this point suspect—since it never reaches a conclusion except by eliminating one of the impulses that has, in varying degrees, contributed to its formation—and if comprehending is nothing other than a precarious armistice between obscure forces, then, out of this concern for integrity that directs Nietzsche's investigation so as to bring more consciousness to our impulsive forces, comprehending can act only by exercising a perpetual complicity with our tendencies, good or bad. However, does it not seem that this illusion is worse than the one for which Nietzsche reproached Spinoza, when Spinoza opposed the act of comprehending to the fact of laughing, crying, and hating? How can an obscure force reach consciousness as an obscure force if it does not already belong to the full light of consciousness? As the Apostle said, "*All things that are condemned are made manifest by the light, for whatever makes manifest is light.*"[13] How to *manifest without condemning*? How can an obscure force be made manifest without condemning itself to be illuminated? Could there not be a light that is not a condemnation of the shadows? Pathos knows, no doubt, but we cannot share in its mode of knowing except through this condemnation: "Take no part in the unfruitful works of the shadows," said the Apostle.[14] Nevertheless, it is written that "*the light shines in the darkness, but the darkness did not receive it.*"[15] The light wanted to be received by the shadows; there is thus a moment when the light is a condemnation, and there is *a moment when the light seeks to be received by the shadows.*

Everything that rises up into the full light of consciousness rises up upside down—the images of night are reversed in the mirror of conscious thought. Later we will see that there is a necessity deeply inscribed in the law of being that is explicated as the universal wheel, the image of eternity—and that the results of this law is the inversion of night into day, and of sleep into the wakefulness of consciousness. Conscious thought is constituted only in and through an ignorance of this law of return. Every conscious thought looks forward, identifying itself with a goal that it posits before itself as its own definition. But if conscious thought tends to invert the images of the night in full day, this is because, in taking exteriority as a point of departure, it claims to be *speaking*, even as it mistranslates an original text of which it is unaware. As Nietzsche says:

"Consciousness does not really belong to man's individual existence. . . . The *thinking* that rises to *consciousness* is only a tiny part of ourselves—the most superficial and worst part—for only this conscious thinking *takes the form of words*, which is to say, *signs of communication.* . . . The emergence of our sense impressions into our own consciousness, the ability to fix them and, as it were, exhibit them externally, increased proportionally with the need to communicate them to *others* by means of signs. . . . Consciousness has developed subtlety only insofar as this is required by social or herd utility. Consequently, given the best will in the world to understand ourselves as individually as possible, 'to know ourselves,' each of us will only succeed in becoming conscious only of what is not individual but 'average.' . . . Fundamentally, all our actions are altogether incomparably personal, unique, and infinitely individual; there is no doubt of that. But as soon as we translate them into consciousness *they no longer seem to be.*"[16] In conclusion: every coming to consciousness is the result of an operation of generalization, of falsification, and thus is a fundamentally ruinous operation.

"It is not the opposition of subject and object that concerns me here: this distinction I leave to the epistemologists who have become entangled in the snares of grammar (the metaphysics of the people). It is even less the opposition of 'thing-in-itself' and appearance; for we do not 'know' nearly enough to be entitled to any such distinction. We simply lack any organ for knowledge, for 'truth': we 'know' (or believe or imagine) just as much as may be *useful* in the interests of the human herd, the species; and even what is here called 'utility' is ultimately also a mere belief, something imaginary, and perhaps precisely that most calamitous stupidity of which we shall perish someday."[17]

According to this definition, what conscious thought produces is always only the most utilizable part of ourselves, because only that part is communicable; what we have of the most essential part of ourselves will thus remain an incommunicable and non-utilizable pathos.

By the individual, by the personal, by the most essential part of ourselves, Nietzsche in no way means what is generally understood by the term "individualism." We will see, on the contrary, that the individual and the non-individual will be linked in an indiscernible unity, which is indicated by this very concern for the authentic. But here we encounter a number of difficulties in Nietzsche.

If conscious thought inevitably betrays what we have of the most essential part of ourselves, how can this essential aspect be communicated to us? How can it be distinguished from the gregarious and, since the gregarious is always tainted by the pejorative notion of utility, how will this essential aspect of ourselves escape our own utilitarian thought? Will what is authentic in us be something entirely useless in its integrity, and thus properly valuable in Nietzsche's sense, such that here we at last find an apprehension of existence that is sufficient in itself, a possibility of being both *One and All?*

For conscious thought—the so-called gregarious thought that reveals nothing essential of ourselves, the thought disqualified by Nietzsche—the greatest distress is to remain without a goal, for example, the absence of a truth to be sought for and attained as the supreme goal of conscious thought. By its nature and by definition, conscious thought in itself is always projecting itself forward in search of a goal.

On the other hand, the greatest pleasure of our pathos—the unconscious life of the impulses, the essential aspect of ourselves—is to be without *any* goal. Inversely, if the belief in a goal makes consciousness happier and procures a degree of security for conscious thought, the effect of this assignation of an end is felt (or can be felt) in our pathos only as the greatest distress. When Nietzsche critiques Spinoza, he means nothing other than this. For although the impulses as needs are obviously unaware of what consciousness wants, they nevertheless imagine that of which they are themselves the need. As soon as consciousness posits a goal, the impulses momentarily lose this image they have of themselves. As images of themselves, the impulses are alienated from their own image for the benefit of the goal—of which they are, by nature, unaware.

If the essential aspect of ourselves lies in our pathos—which is inexpressible or incommunicable by itself—then insofar as it forms the ensemble of our impulsive life, it also constitutes an ensemble of needs. But does it not then seek to satisfy itself in its own dissipation [*dépense*]?[18] And how would this dissipation effect itself and find satisfaction? When our deepest need expresses the most essential part of ourselves in laughter and tears, for example, it would dissipate itself as laughing and crying, which are in themselves the image of this need. The laughing and crying would be produced independently of any motive that conscious thought would attribute to them, rightly or wrongly, from its goal-oriented perspective. And being thus dissipated, our most profound need and the loss of any goal would coincide, for an instant, with our profound happiness.

Even when we do not know how to share its mode of understanding, our pathos does not thereby prevent us from understanding ourselves. For where do such sudden satisfactions, coupled with the absence of any rational motive, come from—for instance, when I laugh or cry, seemingly without reason, before some spectacle such as those offered by the view of a suddenly discovered landscape or of tidal pools at the edge of the ocean? Something is laughing or crying in us that, by making use of us, is robbing us of ourselves and concealing us from ourselves, but which, by making use of us, is concealing itself. Does this mean that this something was not *present* otherwise than in the tears and laughter? For if I laugh and cry in this way, I take myself to be expressing nothing but the immediate vanishing of this unknown motive, which has found in me neither figure nor sense, apart from the image of this forest or these waves greedy for buried treasures. In relation to this unknown motive, which is hidden from me by these outward images, I am, in Nietzsche's sense, only a *fragment*, an *enigma* to myself, *a horrifying chance*. And I will remain a *fragment*, an *enigma*, and a *chance* in relation to that most essential aspect of myself, which speaks through this laughter and these tears without any rational motive. But this most essential aspect of myself, which is made manifest in this way, corresponds to an image hidden in the full light of consciousness, an image that appears to me as inverted and that arrives late in the goal-oriented perspective, which wants to lend as much consciousness as possible to this laughter or to these tears. Thus there must be a necessity that wills me to laugh or cry as if I were crying or laughing freely. But is not this *necessity* the very *same* necessity that inverts night into day, which inverts sleep into the wakefulness where consciousness posits its goal? Is this not the same necessity that will re-invert the images of the day into those of night? To live and to think in the goal-oriented perspective is to distance myself from what is most essential in me, or from the necessity that testifies, within me, to my deepest need. To want to recuperate this most essential part of myself amounts to living backwards from my consciousness, and therefore *I will put all my will and confidence in the necessity that has made me laugh and cry without any motive.* For the movement that throws consciousness out of the night and into the dawn, where it posits its goal, is the same movement that carries me far from this goal in order to lead me back, at deepest midnight, to what I have that is most essential. To suffer this necessity is one thing; it is quite another thing to adhere to it as a law, and still another thing to formu-late this law in the image of a circle.

We have seen that the aspiration to truth is given to us as an impulse, and that this impulse becomes identified with the function of consciousness. Consequently, to ask whether the aspiration to truth can be assimilated to pathos and its errors amounts to asking whether pathos can produce some-thing that it must still assimilate. Thus, if consciousness simply pursues this aspiration as its own impulse, by this very fact that impulse works toward its own ruin in the name of truth. What is this thing that pursues such an impulsive aspiration, this thing or this state of things that consciousness posits, in the full light of day, under the name of truth and as its own end? What is this word "truth" if not the inverted image of what produced this impulse to truth as a need? To re-invert this ultimate impulse called the "aspiration to truth"—this aspiration of the totality of pathos taken together—to re-invert the image of this aspiration would come down to for-mulating what Nietzsche states in the following proposition: "*Truth is an error without which a certain species of life could not live. The value for life is ulti-mately decisive.*"[19] The most recent aspiration that has come to life—this dangerous aspiration to truth—is nothing other than the return of pathos in its totality in the form of a goal.

But here we discover something disquieting in Nietzsche. What did he mean by posing the question of knowing if *truth could endure its incorporation as a condition of life*? What did he mean by saying that the *impulsive aspiration to truth* had become *life-preserving* at the same time as the *natural errors*? Are not these questions asked from the viewpoint of conscious and gregarious thought, that is, in the terms of the very consciousness that necessarily gives itself a goal? And would not the terms "error" and "truth," which had previously been emptied of their gregarious meaning, immediately be filled again with this same content?

For the philosopher (or the thinker or the sage in the Nietzschean sense), the question is: "What form could be given to this experience so that it could be taught?" How could the will be persuaded to will the opposite of every goal given by conscious thought, such that the will could strive to recuperate its most essential and least communicable aspect? How could the will be persuaded to take itself as its own object, thereby producing an apprehension of existence returning to itself just as the will returns to itself? Was it not necessary to appeal to conscious thought, and thus to borrow from the language of the herd (in this case, the language of positivism), and thus to take up once again the notions of utility and goal, and direct them toward and against every utility, toward and against every goal?

In his retrospective preface to *The Gay Science*, dated 1886, we read:

"'Incipit tragedia' *is written at the end of this book, with a disquieting casualness—Beware! Something downright wicked and malicious is announced here:* incipit parodia."[20]

"*What is the meaning,*" Nietzsche asks in the first aphorism of *The Gay Science,* "*what is the meaning of the ever new appearance of these founders of moralities and religions . . . these teachers of remorse and religious wars? What is the meaning of these heroes on this stage? . . . It is obvious that these tragedians, too, promote the interest of God or work as God's emissaries. They, too, promote the life of the species by promoting the faith in life. 'Life is worth living,' every one of them shouts; 'there is something to life, there is something behind life, beneath it; beware! From time to time this instinct, which is at work equally in the highest and basest men—the instinct for the preservation of the species—erupts as reason and as passion of the spirit. Then it is surrounded by a resplendent retinue of reason and tries with all the force at its command to make us forget that at bottom it is instinct, drive, folly, lack of reasons. Life shall be loved, because—! Man shall advance himself and his neighbor, because—! . . .* In order that what happens necessarily and always, spontaneously and without any purpose, may henceforth appear to be done for some purpose and strike man as rational and an ultimate commandment, the ethical teacher comes on the stage, as the teacher of the purpose of existence; and to this end he invents a second, different existence and unhinges by means of his new mechanics the old, ordinary existence." And Nietzsche concludes: "*Not only laughter and gay wisdom but the tragic, too, with all its sublime unreason, belongs among the means and necessities of the preservation of the species. Consequently—. Consequently. Consequently. O, do you understand me, my brothers? Do you understand this new law of ebb and flood? There is a time for us, too!*"[21]

Does this mean that Nietzsche in turn would like to enter the stage as a new doctor of the goal of existence? As a new doctor of morality? Does this mean that, in order to come to the aid of the most essential aspect of ourselves, we must inevitably appeal to the rationalizations of conscious thought and the positing of a goal—even though it is a question of apprehending an existence without a goal? Nietzsche always has a formula that seems to imply an imperative: the will to power.

This entails a serious question: what is Nietzsche's true language? Is it the language of lived experience, or of inspiration, or of revelation, or perhaps of the experiment to be performed, the language of experimentation? Is there not, in each case, an interference between these various languages, which intervenes in the desire to legitimate the incommunicable lived experience of the eternal return by way of a demonstration? Does not Nietzsche provide this demonstration at the level of the scientifically verifiable cosmos—and on the moral plane, by elaborating an imperative that can command the will under its relation to the will to power? Is this not the point where the dubious references to science and biology intervene, when Nietzsche's fundamental experience is already being expressed on an entirely different level by the character of Zarathustra? Perhaps we have here one of the alternating terms, one of the aspects of Nietzsche's antinomy: the experience of the eternity of the self at the ecstatic moment of the eternal return of all things could not be the object of an experimentation any more than it could be the object of a rationally constructed elucidation; any more than the lived, inexpressible, and therefore incommunicable experience could ground an ethical imperative that would turn the *lived* into something *willed* and a *rewilled*, insofar as the universal movement of the eternal return is supposed to lead the will to will infallibly at *the willed moment*. The lived experience is thus entirely implicit in a *contemplation* where the will is completely absorbed in an existence rendered to itself—so that the will to power is simply an attribute of existence, which wills itself only insofar as it *is*. This explains the often doubtful character of those propositions of Nietzsche's, in the fragments on the *transvaluation of values*, that consider will to power independently of the law of the eternal return, independently of this revelation from which it is inseparable. At the level of lived experience, Nietzsche is already surpassed by his own *Zarathustra*. Nietzsche is no more than the doctor of a counter-morality that is seemingly expressed in clear language, and whose worth comes from this audacious use of conscious thought for the benefit of that which has no goal. He is the doctor of a goal for existence, charged with covering up his own retreat into that region where, in reality, he has already retired—this immortality from which he has perished, as he says more than once, and from which he will return in delirious transports to show what he is under two different names: Dionysus and the Crucified.

After the proposition: *Truth is a necessary error*, we find this other proposition: *Art is a higher value than truth*, which is the conclusion of those propositions which declare that *art prevents us from losing ourselves in the truth* or *art protects us from the truth*. All these propositions have the same pragmatic character as the preceding proposition: *truth is only a necessary error*[22]—a character that holds precisely because everything is being considered solely from the viewpoint of its usefulness.

Nevertheless, as soon as *error* creates *forms*, it goes without saying that art must effectively become that domain where *willed error* inaugurates a *rule of the game*. Just as it is contradictory to give a practical application of truth as error, so it appears that, in this domain of the game *par excellence* which is art, imposture constitutes a legitimate activity in accord with the reason of fiction. But art has a very wide meaning, and in Nietzsche, this category includes institutions as much as works of free creation. For example—and here we can see immediately what is at issue—how does Nietzsche consider the Church? For him, the Church is constituted *grosso modo* by a cast of *profound impostors*: the priests. The Church is a masterpiece of spiritual domination, and it required that impossible plebian monk, Luther, to dream of ruining that masterpiece, the last edifice of Roman civilization among us. The admiration Nietzsche always had for the Church and the papacy rests precisely upon the idea that truth is an error, and that art, as *willed error*, is higher than truth. This is why Zarathustra confesses his affinity with the priest, and why, in the Fourth Part, during that extraordinary gathering of the different kinds of higher men in Zarathustra's cave, the Pope—the Last Pope—is one of the prophet's guests of honor.[23] This betrays, I think, Nietzsche's temptation to foresee a ruling class of great *meta-psychologists* who would take charge of the destinies of future humanity, since they would know perfectly both the different aspirations and the different resources capable of satisfying them. What interests us, however, is a particular problem that never ceased to preoccupy Nietzsche: the problem of the actor. We read in aphorism 361 of *The Gay Science*: "*Falseness with a good conscience; the delight in simulation exploding as a power that pushes aside one's so-called 'character,' flooding it and at times extinguishing it; the inner craving for a role and mask, for* appearance; *an excess of the capacity for all kinds of adaptations that can no longer be satisfied in the service of the most immediate and narrow utility—all of this is perhaps not only peculiar to the actor.*"[24]

Let us take careful note of everything Nietzsche is revealing here: *delight in simulation exploding as a power; pushing aside one's so-called "character," submerging it sometimes to the point of extinguishing it*—here we suddenly perceive what was threatening Nietzsche himself: first of all, simulation exploding as power to the point of submerging or extinguishing one's so-called "character." The point here is that simulation is not only a means but also a *power*—and thus that there is an *irruption* of something incompatible with one's so-called "character," a putting into question of what one is in a situation that has been determined by this same indeterminable. Nietzsche calls this putting into question *a surplus of the adaptive faculties*, but this surplus, he remarks, *never manages to satisfy itself*, or *to serve an immediate and strict utility*. This is why *that which* is expressed by thus surplus of the faculties of adaptation has a role, which is *existence itself*—existence without a goal, existence sufficient unto itself. But let us return, once again, to the first line: *falseness with a good conscience*. Here we confront anew the notion of the *willed error*. In the rationality of simulacra, it is *willed error* that provides an account of that existence whose very essence lies in the truth that conceals itself, that refuses itself.

Existence seeks a physiognomy in order to reveal itself; the actor is its medium. What reveals existence? A possible physiognomy: perhaps that of a god.

In another curious passage from *The Gay Science* (aphorism 356), entitled "*How things will become ever more 'artistic' in Europe*," Nietzsche remarks that the care to make a living compels almost all Europeans to adopt a particular role, their "occupation." Some people manage to retain the merely apparent freedom of choosing this role for themselves, while for most people it is prescribed in advance. The result is quite singular: almost everyone identifies themselves with their role—*everyone forgets at what point chance, disposition, and arbitrariness were at work in them* when the question of their so-called "vocation" was decided—and how many other roles they might perhaps have been *able* to play, although now it is too late. *In a more profound sense, the role has actually become character, and art has become nature.* Later, the same aphorism discusses the question of social degradation, but what I would like to emphasize is this: what is here described as a phenomenon of contemporary social life appears in reality as the image of destiny itself—and of Nietzsche's destiny in particular. We believe we choose freely to be what we are, but not being what *we are*, we are in fact constrained to play a role—and thus to play the role of what *we are outside ourselves*. We are never where *we are*, but always where we are only the actor of *this other* that *we are*. The role represents the fortuitousness in the necessity of destiny. We cannot not will, but we can never will something other than a role. To know this is to play *in good conscience*, and to play as well as possible amounts to dissimulating oneself. Thus, to be a *professor of philology at Basel* or even the *author of Zarathustra* is nothing other than to play a *role*. What one dissimulates is the fact that one is nothing other than existence, and one dissimulates the fact that the role one plays refers to existence itself.

This problem of the actor in Nietzsche, and this irruption of a power in a so-called "character" that threatens to submerge it to the point of extinguishing it—this problem, I am saying, is immediately relevant to Nietzsche's own identity, to the putting in question of this identity considered as fortuitously received and then taken on as a role—just as the role someone chooses to play can be rejected as a mask in favor of another one from among the thousands of masks of history. Having produced this conception from the valorization of the *willed error*, the valorization of imposture as a simulacrum, it now remains to determine to what extent the simulacrum, if it is an apprehension of existence, constitutes a manifestation of being in the existent being—a manifestation of being in the fortuitous existent.

Is existence still capable of a God? asks Heidegger. This question is asked as much in the biographical context of the person who formulates it for the first time as a piece of news—*God is dead*—as it is asked in the context of the events and the thought of the contemporary epoch.

The day after his collapse, in Turin, Nietzsche awakens with the feeling of being both Dionysus and the Crucified, and he signs the letters he sends to Strindberg, Burckhardt, and other notable figures with one of these divine names.

Until this point, it had always been a matter of opposing Dionysus and the Crucified: "*Have I been understood? Dionysus versus the Crucified.*"[25] Now that Nietzsche the professor has faded—or rather, now that he has finally abolished all limits between outside and inside—he declares that the *two gods* are living together in him. Let us distance ourselves from all questions of pathology, and retain this declaration as a valid judgment of his own apprehension of existence. The substitution of the divine names for that of "Nietzsche" immediately touches upon the problem of the identity of the person in relation to *a single God*, who is the truth, and to the existence of many gods, insofar as they are the explication of being, on the one hand, and an expression of the plurality within a single individual, within each and every individual, on the other.

Thus Nietzsche maintains within himself the image of Christ, or rather, as he says, of the Crucified, a supreme symbol that remains in him as the indispensable opposite of Dionysus. Through their very antagonism, the two names "Christ" and "Dionysus" constitute an equilibrium.

It is clear that this brings us back to the problem of the authentic incommunicable. It is in this context that Karl Löwith, in his important book on the eternal return, poses the following question of credibility to Nietzsche's doctrine: If he is not Dionysus, does not the whole edifice fall into ruin?[26] But I am claiming that this question does not see in what sense the simulacrum can or cannot give an account of the authentic.

When Nietzsche announces that *God is dead*, this amounts to saying that Nietzsche must necessarily lose his own identity. What is presented here as an ontological catastrophe corresponds exactly to the reabsorption of both the true world and apparent world into the fable. Within the fable, there is a plurality of norms; or rather, there is no norm at all properly speaking, because the very principle of a responsible identity is unknown in the fable, insofar as existence is neither clarified nor revealed in the physiognomy of a unique God who, as the judge of a responsible self, would extract the individual from a potential plurality.

God is dead does not mean that the divinity ceases to act as a clarification of existence, but rather that the absolute guarantee of the identity of the responsible self vanishes from the horizon of Nietzsche's consciousness, which in turn merges with this disappearance.

If the concept of identity vanishes, at first sight all that remains is the fortuitousness that befalls consciousness. Up until then, consciousness recognized the fortuitous by virtue of its apparently necessary identity, which judges that all things around it are either necessary or fortuitous.

But, as soon as the fortuitous is revealed to consciousness as the necessary effect of a universal law, as the wheel of fortune, it can consider itself to be fortuitous. All that remains for consciousness is to declare that its own identity is a fortuitous case arbitrarily maintained as necessary, even if this means understanding itself through this universal wheel of fortune, and even if this means embracing (if possible) the totality of cases, fortuitousness itself in its necessary totality.

What subsists then is being, and the verb "to be" is never applicable to being itself, but to the fortuitous. In Nietzsche's declaration, "*I am Chambige, I am Badinguet, I am Prado. . . . At bottom I am every name in history*,"[27] we can see his consciousness enumerating, like so many drawings in a lottery, the different possibilities of being that, taken together, would be being itself. These different possibilities make use of the momentary success that is named Nietzsche, but who, as a success, winds up abdicating himself for a more generous demonstration of being. "*In the end I would much rather be a Basel professor than God; but I have not dared push my personal egoism so far as to desist for its sake from the creation of the world. . . . One must make sacrifices however and wherever one lives.*"[28]

Existence as the eternal return of all things is produced in the physiognomies of as many multiple gods as it has possible manifestations in the souls of men. If the will adheres to this perpetual movement of the universe, what it contemplates is first the wheel of the gods, as it is said in *Zarathustra*:

> The universe is only an eternal-fleeing-from-itself, an eternal-returning-into-itself of multiple gods, a blessed-contradicting, a blessed-reconciling, a rejoining of multiple gods.[29]

No doubt, the Nietzschean version of polytheism is necessarily as distant from the devotion of antiquity as his concept of a divine instinct generating many gods is necessarily distant from the Christian notion of divinity. But what this "version" shows is the refusal to settle into an atheistic morality that, for Nietzsche, was no less suffocating than the monotheistic morality. He could not help but see in atheistic and humanistic morality merely the continuation of what he felt was the tyranny of a unique truth, whatever its name might be—whether it appeared in the form of a categorical imperative or as the physiognomy of an exclusive and personal God. Thus, the disbelief in a unique and normative God, in a God who is the Truth, is nonetheless affirmed as an *impiety that is divinely inspired*, which forbids any refolding of reason back into strictly human limits. Nietzschean impiety not only discredits rational man, but remains complicit with all the phantasms that are reflections in the soul of everything that man has had to expel in order to arrive at a rational definition of his nature. This impiety, however, does not aspire to a pure and simple unleashing of blind forces, as some are often led to say with regard to Nietzsche. He has nothing in common with a vitalism that would make a clean slate of all of the elaborated forms of culture. Nietzsche is at the antipodes of any naturalism, and his impiety declares itself to be a tributary of his culture. This is why one finds, in Zarathustra's incantation, something like an appeal to an insurrection of images—those images that the human soul is able to form, in its phantasms, from its own obscure forces. These phantasms testify to the soul's aptitude for an always-inexhaustible metamorphosis, its need for an unappeasable and universal investment, in which various diverse extrahuman forms of existence are offered to the soul as so many possibilities of being—stone, plant, animal, star—but precisely insofar as they would always be possibilities for the life of the soul itself. This aptitude for metamorphosis (which, under the regime of an exclusive normative principle, is one of the major temptations that man has had to struggle against for millennia in order to conquer and define himself) has not itself contributed to the eliminatory formation that had to lead to man. The proof of this can be found in the delimitation of the divine and the human, and in that admirable compensation by which man—to the extent that he renounces his bestiality, vegetality, and minerality, and hierarchizes his desires and passions according to always-variable criteria—reveals within himself an analogous hierarchy in regions that are supra- or infraworldly. The universe is populated by many divinities, by various divinities of both sexes, and thus divinities that are capable of pursuing, fleeing from, and uniting with each other. So it was at that moment when the surprising equilibrium of the world blossomed into myth, when—thanks to the simulacra of multiple gods, diverse with regard to their gender and sex[ii]—neither "conscious" nor

---

ii. What is glimpsed here is not the return of a demonology (*obscure forces* as *demons*) but a *theogony* (psychic dispositions as divinities; antagonistic and conciliatory dispositions as divinities given to quarreling and coupling). The demonology of Neoplatonic origin was already tending toward a psychology, a kind of figurative psychology. Pan-theology, on the other hand, presupposes a *notion of space* where the inner life of the soul and the life of the cosmos form a single space, in which the event—which, for us, is "psychological"—is situated as a spatial fact. This is why the pan-theology of *myth*—with its *genealogies* of divinities, its *amorous adventures* of gods and goddesses—creates an equilibrium between man and his own forces, for the latter find their physiognomies in the eternal figure of the gods. The practical consequences of such an equilibrium are the exact opposite of those that follow from a purely psychological conception—that is, conscience and the will, and hence the morality of behavior. In a *theogony*, what reigns is simply an exchange or commerce between the favor and disfavor of being: the physiognomy of some god who attracts or repulses the physiognomy of some goddess, according to the rule of the law of the chase, of erotic attraction. However, *this is not* what we have been led to call a *pure transposition* of human experience, but rather a process that belongs to the very manifestations of being:

"unconscious," neither "outside" nor "inside," neither "obscure forces" nor "phantasms" preoccupied the mind, once the entire soul managed to situate these images in space, and to render them indistinguishable from the soul. Out of this relation between the divine and the human, moral monotheism has achieved the conquest of man by himself, and has subjugated nature to man by enabling the anthropological phenomenon of science. Moreover, according to Nietzsche, after two millennia this relation has provoked that profound disequilibrium which has resulted in the disarray of nihilism. Hence the alienation of the universe from man, which Nietzsche discerned in the exploration of the universe by science; and hence the loss of what is expressed by this nostalgia for the soul (as capable of metamorphosis): the fundamental *eros* that makes man, as Nietzsche says, *the animal who reveres*.[30] What becomes apparent, then, is that the event of the "death of God" stirs the *eros* of the soul at its root; it awakens the instinct of adoration, this *instinct that generates gods*, which in Nietzsche is both a *creative will* and a *will to eternalization*.[31] The "death of God" means that a rupture is introduced into this *eros*, which is then split into two contrary tendencies: the *will to self-creation*, which is never without destruction, and the *will to adore*, which is never willed without willing eternalization. Insofar as the *will to power* is simply another term for this set of tendencies and constitutes the universal capacity for metamorphosis, it finds something of a compensation, or a kind of healing, in its identification with *Dionysus*, in the sense that, in Nietzsche, this ancient god of polytheism would express and combine within himself all the dead and resurrected gods.

Zarathustra himself accounts for the dissociation of these two willings (the will to create and the will to adore) when he demands the creation of new values—and thus new truths, which man would not know how to either believe or obey, since they would be marked with the seal of distress and destruction. It would be impossible for the will to create new values to ever appease the need to adore, since this need is implicit in the will to eternalization of oneself. If man is an animal that reveres, he would only know how to revere what comes to him from the necessity of being—by virtue of which he cannot not will to be. For this reason, he would not know how to either obey or believe in the values he deliberately creates, were it not a matter of the very simulacra of his need for eternity. Hence the alternation, in Zarathustra, between the *will to create*, in the absence of gods, and the contemplation of the *dance of the gods*, which explains the universe. It is when he

---

the commerce of the sexes in the form of divinities is simply an explication of being in its modes of *appearing* and *disappearing*, whereas in its human form this same exchange is simply the experience of living and dying. What we call theogony is nothing other than a necessary participation in the explications of being in divine physiognomies.

announces that *all the gods are dead* that Zarathustra demands that what must now *live* is the overman, that is, a humanity that knows how to overcome itself. How is it overcome? By rewilling that everything that already was be reproduced, and to do this as its own activity. This act is defined as the will to create: as Zarathustra declares, *"if there were gods, what would there be to create?"*[32] But what is it that leads man to create if not the law of the eternal return, to which he decides to adhere? To what does he adhere if not a life that he has *forgotten*, but which the revelation of the eternal return as law incites him to re-will? And what does he re-will if not that which he now does not want to will? Is this to say that the absence of gods incites him to create new gods? Or does he want to prevent the return of those ages when he adored the gods? In re-willing the gods, does he make man move to a higher life? But how would this life be a higher life, if it tends toward that which already was? In other words, how could it be a higher life if it tends toward a state where it does not want to create, but would rather adore the gods? Once again, it would thus seem that the doctrine of the eternal return is conceived as a *simulacrum of a doctrine*, whose parodic character gives an account of *hilarity* as an attribute of existence—an attribute that becomes sufficient to itself when laughter bursts from the ground [*fond*] of the whole truth, either because the truth explodes in the laughter of the gods, or because the gods themselves die from a mad laughter.

When a god wanted to be the only God, all the other gods were seized by a mad laughter, to the point where they died laughing.[33]

For what is the divine, if not the fact that there are many gods and not a single God?

Laughter is here like the supreme image, the supreme manifestation of the divine reabsorbing the announced gods, and announcing the gods with a new burst of laughter; for if the gods are dying from this laughter, it is also from *this laughter that bursts from the ground of the whole truth* that the gods are reborn.

We must follow Zarathustra to the end of his adventure in order to see the refutation of this need to create for and against necessity, which *denounces* the *solidarity* between the three forces of *eternalization, adoration,* and *creation*—the three cardinal virtues in Nietzsche. In this refutation, we can see that the death of God and the distress of the fundamental eros, the distress of the need to revere (a distress that the *will to create* turns from in derision as its own failure), are identical. For if it is the failure of a single instinct, the derision that compensates for it is nonetheless inscribed in the necessity of the eternal return. Once he has willed the eternal return of all things, Zarathustra has chosen in advance to see his own doctrine turned from in derision, as if *laughter, that infallible murderer*, were both the best inspirer of the doctrine as well as its best denigrator. *Thus the eternal return of all things also wills the return of the gods*. What other meaning than this can be attributed to the extraordinary parody of the Communion, in which God's murderer is also the person who offers the chalice to the ass: a sacrilegious figure of the Christian God from pagan times, but more specifically a sacred animal in the ancient mysteries, the *Golden* Ass of the Isiac[34] initiation, an animal worthy of its tireless "Ia!"[iii]— its tireless *yes* lets all things return—worthy of representing the long-suffering of the divine, worthy also of incarnating an ancient divinity, Dionysus, the god of the vine, resurrected in general drunkenness. Thus, finally, as the Wanderer tells Zarathustra: *"in the case of gods, death is always a mere prejudice."*[35]

---

iii. Ia: *ita est!* [The refrain of the ass during the "Ass Festival" in Part IV of *Thus Spoke Zarathustra*, pp. 425–436. "Ita est" is Latin meaning, literally, "it is indeed." Kaufmann renders it as "Yea-Yuh."—trans.]

Translator's Afterword

Klossowski's *salto mortale*

Such a Deathly Desire was originally published in 1963 and collects together seven essays that had previously appeared in diverse publications during the preceding fifteen years. Appended to these essays is an eighth, longer essay, "Nietzsche, Polytheism, and Parody," that was given as a lecture in 1957 but had not previously appeared in print. The work was Klossowski's first major theoretical work since the publication of *Sade, My Neighbor* in 1947. Between the two works, Klossowski had published his trilogy, *The Laws of Hospitality*, whose final volume, *Le Souffleur ou la Théâtre de société*, appeared in 1960. Most of the essays included in the volume have been reworked, in some cases (such as the essay on Blanchot) substantially. This reediting, as well as the fact that the book does not preserve the chronology of the original publication of the essays, is evidence of the thematic unity of the work. A key indication of these themes can be found in the title of the book: a line from Klossowski's now infamous translation of Virgil's *Aeneid*.[1]

In the Fifth Book of Virgil's epic, Aeneas and his companions arrive (again) in Sicily, having fled the destruction of their native Troy, hounded by Juno, and having just left Dido, the queen of Carthage, to despair and consequent suicide for her love of Aeneas. Their arrival coincides with the anniversary of the death of Aeneas' father, Anchises, who is buried on Sicily (where the Trojans had previously landed, the circularity of their voyage serving to further emphasize the despair that grips them upon their return). In commemoration of his father, Aeneas presides over a series of games and contests but, as they celebrate, the Trojan women, weeping over their fate, are driven by an agent of Juno to set fire to the ships pulled up on shore in an effort to bring an end to their pursuit of Italy's shores. Torn as to whether to continue his voyage after this display of despair, Aeneas is visited by Anchises' shade who tells him to undertake a journey to the Underworld in order to receive his counsel.

Aeneas sets forth from Sicily with his best men and, upon landing in Italy, goes to meet the Sibyl who will reveal the way to the Underworld. The priestess, gripped by Apollo, sings of the violence and toil that the Trojans will face in Italy as they struggle to found their new city. Aeneas brushes this aside—having himself foreseen it—and presses the Sibyl to tell him what is required for him to reach Anchises. The Sibyl tells him that he must perform two tasks: obtain a golden bough for Persephone, and provide a proper burial for one of the Trojans who was washed overboard and killed during the passage from Sicily to Italy. Aeneas completes both tasks and follows the Sibyl into the Underworld. Passing through the shadows of monstrous beasts and the crowds of unburied dead, Aeneas leaves the golden bough at the gate of Hades' palace before going on to Elysium, where he is greeted by the sight of the souls of the blessed ranging over a beautiful plain bounded on one side by a large river, sporting and acting as though they still lived. Finding Anchises, Aeneas asks his father's shade about the other shades and the river, Lethe. Anchises tells him that Lethe's waters are those of forgetfulness which strip a soul of mortal cares and desires and ready it to assume a new body. Struck that anyone would ever willingly leave Elysium, Aeneas asks Anchises, "*quae lucis miseris tam dira cupido?*" Roughly: "what is this so deathly desire that these wretched ones have for light?"[2]

In answer, Anchises weaves a cosmology in which, according to the action of mind [*nous*], a great living mass is created through the infusion of celestial spirit [*spiritus*] into the corporeal world. From this inspirited matter living things arise, individuals whose activity manifests their celestial origin of spirit even as they are mingled and dampened by the earthly mortality of their flesh. Because of occlusion by the body, these celestial elements of spirit cannot clearly see that after which they strive and their compounded desire becomes mortal passion. So thorough is this mixing that its taint persists in the soul even after the death of the body. All of these afflictions [*pestes*] are then extracted through penance [*poenis*], achieved by the subjection of the soul to elemental forces as well as through the simple passage of time. The shades of Elysium are these purified, celestial elements of spirit and, when they have dwelt in Elysium for a thousand years and regained the purity of their origin, they are called by the god to Lethe, whose waters erase the memories of their body and, through this forgetting, their desire to be embodied is rekindled.

Klossowski's French translation of this forgetful urge of celestial forces to return to the bodies that will necessary constrain them is "*un si funeste désir.*" Significantly, Klossowski chooses the remarkably complex adjective *funeste* to render *dira*, the adjective describing the qualitative force of the cosmos in Anchises' cosmology. *Dira*, when personified [*Dirae*] is the Latin name for the Furies, the goddesses of revenge, and so can be translated as *fearful* or *awful*, but it also originally derives from the language of portents and omens and so carries the sense of *ill-omened, foreboding,* or *dreadful*. In this way it echoes its Greek cognate *deinos*, which means *terrible, awful, divine ruination,* but also simply *godlike*. *Deinos* is also cognate with the Greek verb *daio*, which can mean *to burn* or *to divide* and, in the latter sense, *to divide and distribute lots or destinies*. As an adjective it could be rendered as *fateful*. *Daios*, in turn, meaning *hostile* or *destructive*, is the Doric equivalent of *deios*. The latter term, as well as *deinos*, echo, but have an uncertain etymological relation to *daimon*, the "guiding spirit" most familiar from Socrates' speech in the *Apology*.[3]

Klossowski's choice for rendering *dira*, *funeste* (from the Latin *funestus* meaning *deadly* or *calamitous*) dates from the fourteenth century and is an adjective that attaches to something that causes or is somehow concerned with death. Its primary meaning, according to the Robert, is *mortal* or *finite*. It preserves its etymology in its secondary and tertiary meanings: an adjective that describes a portent of death, something *disastrous*, *tragic*, or *catastrophic*. In literary language it can often carry the sense of *sinister*. Here it is rendered as *deathly* rather than *deadly* because the desire is for mortal life, of which death is a moment.

Deathly certainly does not capture the full richness of the etymological resources that Klossowski makes use of, but even Klossowski does not require *funeste* to do any heavy theoretical lifting. Instead, he coins a new term, *sous-venir* (*à*), compounded of the proposition *sous-* and the verb *venir*. As a proposition or adjective *sous* means *under*, or *beneath*, and is often used in hyphenated expressions to denote not only position but also rank or importance (thus *sous-homme*, *inferior person*). It thus closely corresponds to the English *sub-*. The French verb *venir*, which simply means *to come*, like its English counterparts, has both a spatial (*to approach*) and temporal (*forthcoming*) aspect. Although *sous-venir* would be unfamiliar to Klossowski's French readers, it has a ready antonym in the verb *survenir* (the preposition/prefix *sur-* means *above*) which means *to happen unexpectedly*, while *survenir à* means *to come after* as an addition or supplement. *Sous-venir*, then, would mean the happening of something expected that is not supplementary but essential or integral to the subject of the action. This aspect of the neologism manages to catch the "fateful" aspect of *dira* as well as *funeste*. *Sous-venir* is also a homonym of the common and familiar French word *souvenir*, which can be a verb meaning *to remember*, or a noun meaning either the *faculty of memory* or what the faculty of memory brings to mind, *a memory*. By emphasizing the prefix *sous-*, Klossowski calls attention to, on the one hand, the absence of conscious mastery over the faculty of memory, the way in which consciousness can find itself "submitted" to (literally *placed under*) the power and effects of its remembrances; on the other hand, by echoing a mental faculty, Klossowski indicates that this submission of consciousness in remembrance is not a submission to something accidental or foreign, but to something that is itself an integral part of the mind.[4] *Sous-venir*, then, combining the two aspects, would mean a faculty of remembering to which the conscious mind is necessarily, fatefully, submitted as that which is, ultimately and originally, integral to it. The mind *sub-comes to* (a homonym of *succumbs*) memory when

that memory comes as something unexpected and thereby achieves the submission of consciousness, even as consciousness discovers nothing in this
remembrance or in this faculty other than its own integral nature.

This "*si funeste désir*" is therefore a desire to "sub-come" to the remembrance that is one's fate, one's integral nature. For Virgil, this desire befalls,
as their divine lot, as their fateful destiny, the souls in the Underworld when
they forget the forgetfulness consequent on mortal existence and succumb to
the energetic celestial drive of the primordial spirit.[5] Both Virgil and Klossowski emphasize not the originating character of this spirit, but its perpetual
force which is constituted and sustained by a necessary forgetting. In the
Underworld, what causes Aeneas' surprised exclamation is the apprehension
of the force or power of existence that through the self-forgetfulness of individuals succumbs to its own fateful forgetfulness that renews its desire for
mortal, bodily life, and therefore for its own enervation. What this force of
creation wills, what it aims at so that it can be sustained as the force that it
is, is not the reversal of the conscious enervation of this force—the pollution
that befalls it as a result of its mortal differentiation—but rather the reversal
of the very poles of this judgment on mortal existence. For the living cosmos
to be what it is it cannot forget or eschew mortality, which is the fateful and
fatal aspect of life, but it also cannot simply accept this mortality because it
is antagonistic and antithetical to its own, essentially creative value. Therefore, creation can only accomplish itself in the unconscious reversal of the
reversal that it succumbs to in conscious, mortal life. Those souls that Aeneas
sees succumb to a desire to become mortal precisely because their desire is to
be eternal. They aim at "daylight," the light of day that echoes their finitude,
because they are its integral expression.

Klossowski finds Aeneas' astonishment repeated in "the basic idea of
Zarathustra,"[6] in the question of the demon who poses the question of eternal recurrence: a parable that is decisive not only for Klossowski's reading of
Nietzsche, but for the organization of the theme that runs throughout the
essays of *Such a Deathly Desire*. The question of the demon, insofar as it
invites the discovery of the "secret" of the eternally recurrent will, determines
"the lesson of the *Gaya Scienza*." Klossowski finds Nietzsche's own situation
as an author, his own sub-coming to the moment that is-to-come for him,
expressed in the parable of the demon. As he repeats the insights he gained
concerning history from *On the Advantages and Disadvantages of History for
Life* within himself, as the history of humanity is condensed into the inten-
sive experience of a single soul, Nietzsche's knowledge becomes a power of
metamorphosis.[7] The fundamental question, expressed mythically in the
parable of the demon, is: how can one remember forgetting? How can the
instauration of mortal existence be recollected within that existence itself?
To take on history is to "assimilate" that history, to take it as a plastic resource
of creativity rather than the causal determination of a present state of affairs.

But to find such a resource is precisely to forget the apparent specificity of the willful agent. An individual never remembers forgetting, but a willful agent sub-comes to the eternity of what wills in it insofar as the assimilation and condensation of history is itself a repetition of the eternal plasticity of the force of the celestial will. It is this repetition that is affirmed in the positive response to the demon's question, with the demon serving here as the figuration of the gap between the individual and the celestial will that cannot be overcome or mediated by the finite resources of the former. This is why the affirmative response can only be a "confirmation": it is a choice without understanding, a choice of the will—the only choice the will is capable of alone because it is the only choice that does not require the setting forth of determinate alternatives, itself affirming the distinction of the moment identical to every other moment (the moment of the demon's question) whose identity is precisely the confirmation of the eternal power of willing. The demon, then, on Klossowski's reading, is the image the mind that has discovered the plurality of will must form in order to achieve its own conformity with the law whose recognition forces it into vertiginous forgetfulness. It enables forgetting to be remembered by making forgetting the remembrance of what the individual must disavow in order to be, which is also what that same individual must will in order to become, in order to live and to will. This is the peculiar character of Klossowski's *salto mortale*: not so much a leap as a somersault, a forcing of consciousness through a full circle.

It is the circuit of this *salto mortale*, opened by the question of the demon, that organizes the subsequent essays of the book. In his account of *The Gay Science* and its relation to *On the Advantages and Disadvantages of History for Life*, Klossowski indicates the importance of a certain kind of polytheism for the formation of the image of the demon. Polytheism here can be understood as a new interpretation of the temptation offered by the Serpent in the Garden of Eden. The knowledge to be gained from the proffered fruit is not merely some new piece of information but rather the ability to know multiple truths and multiple norms without judging one to be the negation or refutation of another.[8] Thus Klossowski focuses on Du Bos's reproach to Gide: that the latter's conception of the demon violates the principle of contradiction. However, Klossowski uses Nietzsche's insight into the nature of the demon to uncover a sense for it quite different from the one that Du Bos deploys. According to Tertullian, the demon is not merely a derivative or parasitic entity, but is also an expression of the spiritual as opposed to the bodily and concrete, and such an understanding is at the root of Du Bos's misunderstanding (deliberate or accidental) of Gide. Du Bos takes Gide's invocation of the demon in a transcendental sense, analogous to that of Tertullian, as an invocation to turn away from concrete problems and concerns. Klossowski, however, points out that throughout their exchanges Gide persists in conceiving of the demonic as a matter of the concrete, and also of the freedom of the concrete. Du Bos is therefore right to try to apprehend Gide through the theme of the demon but, precisely because the theme of the simulation of freedom is the very game that Gide is playing, Du Bos becomes lost on his own hunt.

The game is repeated in the correspondence between Gide and Claudel that revolves around their fateful exchange in 1914, on the occasion of Claudel's reading of *The Caves of the Vatican*.[9] Outraged at the novel's pederastic scenes, Claudel demands an explanation, a confession of the meaning and purpose of these themes in his friend's work. Gide obliges him, but attempts to frame the revelation of his own nature in such a way as to elude all of the monstrous identifications that Claudel has already formulated as possibilities. This maneuver forces what is, for Klossowski, a decisive split in the concrete problems instantiated by Gide. Where Gide's life was previously lived through a series of divisions, splittings that again recall Baudelaire's two simultaneous postulates, the exchange with Claudel yields a new pursuit: no longer indexed by the secret that is hidden by its contrary, Gide aims to ruin the notion of identity that permits such a thing as the secret to exist at all. "The secret is equivalent to a psychological and spiritual capitalism, its disclosure to a fungibility of the life of souls."[10] Gide's remarkable and strikingly candid literary output is a function of that demon whose question drives the individual to discover the celestial will whose forgetting enables individuality at all and, for Klossowski, it was in his correspondence that Gide found his demons.[11] Ultimately, then, Gide's project is the dramatization of the demonic interrogation: a performance that places the very notion of the individual in jeopardy and so unites audience and spectacle. This is what allows Klossowski to see in Gide's work the reinvestment of the individual not with a single, unifying divine force, as one reading of Anchises' cosmology might have it, but with the concrete forces that alone yield individuation.

This polytheism, the (re)investment of the individual with the eternal forces of universal metamorphosis, is conjoined to a concern with language in Klossowksi's reading of Barbey d'Aurevilly's *A Married Priest*. Here again, the dramatized will of the individual author achieved through an interlocutor (Barbey's friend Trébutien) serves as the catalyst for the production of a multiple physiognomy. In the case of Barbey, this assumed the form of the dandy, the one who wanted to exalt uselessness as the supreme value and thereby, like Gide, have done with the spiritual capitalism embodied in the economy of the individual and its attendant concepts. Like Sade, whom he echoes in Klossowski's ears, Barbey aims at nothing less than the complete liquidation of moral norms—following the guidance offered by the demon's question—in favor of the triumph or exaltation of "exclusive experiences," idiopathic and idiomatic experiences that permit of no equivalency or exchange. Like Nietzsche, for whom the death of God was an observable fact of the times, Barbey writes amid the divorce of religion and morality and, linking mystery to the

former, seeks to destroy the calculative reason that has yoked itself to the latter. Rather than dismissing him as an eccentric Catholic polemicist, Klossowski finds in Barbey's project the dramatization of the individual who takes
sides against reason and thereby assumes the rhetorical style of orthodoxy. In
A Married Priest the discovery of the death of God yields the same adherence
to rules and prohibitions as belief—the defining form of the individual thereby
perpetually undoes the remembrance of willful forgetfulness.[12]

This collusion with fate is accomplished through the construction of a
literary "edifice" (a term that denotes Barbey's peculiar style) that permits the
reflection of both signs and their ambiguities. The essay on Bataille's *L'Abbé
C* can thus be seen as forming a sort of brief corollary to Klossowski's essay on
A Married Priest. Its title echoing language in its nudity ("L'A, B, C"),
Bataille's story is, for Klossowski, an investigation into the very possibility of
speech engendered by the demonic supposition that the transcendent ground
of language is lost. According to such a suppositioin, it is a seemingly paradoxical fullness of silence that grounds the determinateness of language.
However, this silence only attains normative force in the speech that violates
it. Together with the essays on Parain and Blanchot, this essay situates the
problem of polytheism in language—specifically siting it around the necessity
of the *name* of God. In Bataille's work, all of the apparatus of the Catholic
Church is arrayed in order to express, through the sacrament that exposes the
death of God, the insistent repetition of the name of God within and by language. Language and transgression reflect each other through the reiteration
of the carnal act in language, a reiteration that always *comes too late*, but
whose very untimeliness drives language to its limits (makes it do somer-
saults). This conjunction of the flesh and language is present in Parain's philosophy of language as well. Where Bataille explores the transgressive expressions of language, Parain is concerned with the relation of language and the
body, arguing that the body is created by language and finds its purpose in
conforming to its origin. The fateful, mortal deviation, the division between
the body and its speech, is a sign of the mortal animality of the individual
being. Through these concerns, Klossowski finds Parain taking aim at any
sort of transcendental ego; judgment arises in and as bodily action and, more
important, this action and its judgment occur in a world that is not simply
mastered by it. Language creates the individual by giving it a name that both
indicates the ground of language and the death of that ground. This double
and redoubled fate of language ensures the equality of every speaker and, at
the same time, the inability of any individual judgment to attain legitimacy
in the existent world. The task set for human beings is therefore to formulate
a noncontradictory linguistic expression of that which would guarantee
equality and simultaneously provide an adequate judgment of the world.
Such an idea would be the idea of God—a celestial speech in Anchises' cosmology. Thus Parain links the name of God and the death of the body with

the moment when speech is rendered silent and, at the same time, the moment when the ceaselessness of speech's expression is made manifest beyond the life of the individual. This paradoxical resolution of truth and death organizes Klossowski's reading of Blacnhot's *The Most High*. Reversing Parain, Blanchot contends that mortal language does not end in death but arises there. Language requires a determinate, mortal individual insofar as expression is only ever the image that designates the absence of a thing. Language itself is demonic. The name of God, as the designation of what is undying and never absent, is therefore an absolutely insignificant name, a name for insignificance. Blanchot's novel is a parable of this extreme fatality of language and, ultimately, a continuation of its fateful adventure of expressive signification and significance, which only ever returns to the necessity that what is always must die.

It is fate, *fatum*, that conjoins the vital, celestial will with the mortal, rational will to truth. The expression of this rational will is prediction, the positing of a goal for an action. But every prediction, Klossowski insists, again having recourse to etymology, is also to err, both meanings (and here, remembering Parain, it is a matter of the mortal treason of language) being contained in the Latin *fari*. Prediction, the aspiration of mortal embodiment, is always errant insofar as this aspiration is cloaked in its own mortality and mistakes its individuality for its essence. This antinomy not only cannot be overcome, it is itself constitutive of the highest aspiration of thought: the experience of eternal return. This experience is that of pathos, of the forgetful aspiration of the souls that populate the plain of Lethe, now rendered as the constitutive "impulses" of mortal individuals. Pathos, "the unconscious life of impulses," is what raves as consciousness sub-comes to its own vitality. However, in reflecting on this vital life, consciousness inverts the nature of these very impulses: it forms an image of them as goal-seeking, where the search for a goal is the distinctive mark of *conscious* willing. Stripping this mark away, 'unthinking' consciousness, the impulses are satisfied in what Klossowski calls their "dissipation" (*dépense*). This unconscious life is exposed in moments of vital exuberance (of pain or pleasure) whose intensity is grasped only retrospectively and always with the inkling that this remembering is itself a forgetting of the most essential aspect of the experience. In the accomplishments of pathos, of unconscious impulses, the greatest desires of vitality are satisfied. Insofar as these are the very desires that consciousness sets out to fulfill in its search for truth, consciousness finds its fate in its mortality. As the impulse or will to stabilize the impulses themselves through the determination of the ends or goals of their activity—and this is the will to truth that foretells, that predicts the constancy that will be satisfaction—consciousness in fact wills its dissipation insofar as this dissipation is the accomplishment of the activity of vitality. The will to truth engenders "fabulation" (Klossowski again making use of the etymology of *fari*), the "necessity" of the reversal of the life of consciousness such that the raving of *fatum* which is always apprehended retrospectively could become the object of prediction. This is the circular law of the eternal return. Every prediction is a dramatization of this fatality that can only be experienced.

Truth as willed error—this is the law of thought discovered in Nietzsche—formulated finally as the combative juxtaposition of two gods: "Dionysus versus the Crucified." This is a duality of the one and the many, not of two distinct unities. "Polytheism" expresses the "raving," vital aspect of existence; "God is dead" expresses a liquidation of the guarantor of identity, not its simple transfer (to humanity, for instance). Individual existence becomes fragmentary, fortuitous, when it is discovered as the unstable equilibrium of vital and rational forces. In its aspiration toward stability, toward meaning, and therefore for the attainment of identity, the individual does not come upon but is swept under by the heterogeneous aspirations of the unconscious impulses. Every individual is a perpetual moment—and a *perpetuum mobile* that continues the *salto mortale*—of equilibrium, of creation and the reverence that preserves what is created. The world is thus filled with those gods and goddesses (figures of the forgetful will to mortal externalization) engendered by this equilibrium, deities with as many forms as there are expressions of desirous vitality: jealous, warlike, loving, wrathful, crafty gods capable of unlimited couplings, combinations, and transformations.

However, one might ask whether, in giving expression to the doctrine of eternal return, Nietzsche has not necessarily falsified it by allowing it to be determined according to the language of consciousness, a language with which it is irreconcilable. To use the language of the first aphorism of *The Gay Science*: is Nietzsche condemned to act out the tragedy of the "moral doctor" who obscures the strife of impulsive vitality behind the articulation of a goal (the thought of eternal return) that coordinates every impulsive force around itself. The resolution of this impasse lies in the particular relation between will to power (the impulsive force of celestial vitality) and the experience of eternal return. Taken singly, neither is capable of grounding an imperative or of organizing a meaning. Only when the experience of eternal return is absorbed back into the impulsive flux that is will to power do they attain a degree of consistency. Together, the two principles form Nietzsche's "antinomy," neither one capable of grounding thought. "The lived experience is thus entirely implicit in a *contemplation* where the will is completely absorbed in an existence rendered to itself—so that the will to power is simply an attribute of existence, which wills itself only insofar as it *is*."[13] The mortal will that implicitly posits the limiting errors that it contests with its projects and predictions; and celestial power, the polyphony to which these limits sub-come—both are "absorbed" in the *thought* of eternal return. A "transvaluation of all values," this new thought, as an *experience*, is the parodic inversion of the aspiration to truth.

Because the valorization of willed error is the affirmation of the difficulty encountered by thought in the recoiling of its *salto mortale*, it forms an account of the game of existence played by the finite individual. "We believe we choose freely to be what we are, but not being what *we are*, we are in fact constrained to play a role—and thus to play the role of what *we are outside ourselves*. We are never where *we are*, but always where we are only the actor of *this other* that *we are*."[14] Thus one is fated to play a role—the souls whose lots are drawn must become mortal again—but this fate can be affirmed precisely as a role, as an opportunity for masks to be donned and discarded. To play the actor is to affirm the inversion of consciousness as an inversion and, in so doing, "what one dissimulates is the fact that one is nothing other than existence, and one dissimulates the fact that the role one plays refers to existence itself."[15] This is the case of Nietzsche: the dissimulation of a physician of culture perpetrated by the fortuitous expression of forces.

It cannot be the case that simulation is reducible to an expressive account of the unconscious; such a linguistic avenue has already been closed off. For Klossowski, the disclosive power of the simulation enacted by the mortal will in its affirmative response to the question of the demon is contained in Nietzsche's famous statement: "God is dead." "*God is dead* does not mean that the divinity ceases to act as a clarification of existence, but rather that the absolute guarantee of the identity of the responsible self vanishes from the horizon of Nietzsche's consciousness, which in turn merges with this disappearance."[16] In affirming the sub-coming of the essential part of consciousness, Nietzsche plays at roles to the point that these roles overwhelm any sense of identity. The roles are taken seriously *insofar as they are roles*— no longer in relation to a lost essence—and, in this parody, the fortuitous comes to appear as necessary, as the wheel of fortune (*fatum*).

At the outset of "Nietzsche, Polytheism, and Parody," Klossowski cautions that no other author seems to lead their interpreter to parody them so much as Nietzsche does. Indeed, what could be more inclined to repetition than a thought that conjoins the will to create and the will to revere—the twin temptations of the interpreter? On the one hand is a will to fill the lacunae, to reconcile the apparent contradictions, to orient and subsume the author's work to a single purpose or thesis; on the other, a will to celebrate the insights that ring true and excoriate those that ring false, to prioritize the passages that are, for the interpreter, those that are most deeply affecting, to singularize the insights or blunders even as they are repeated, to revere or to condemn (which itself is merely an inversion of reverence) under the guise of critical engagment. The very title of the essay signals Klossowski's acknowledgement of this bind, and his persistence ensures his parody. But this very acknowledgment voids the essay's pretensions to singularity, its own prejudices. It thus concludes with laughter—the voice of an ass, repeated, and serving as the affirmative seal of the pathos implicated within its thesis.

Notes

CHAPTER ONE. ON SOME FUNDAMENTAL
THEMES OF NIETZSCHE'S *GAYA SCIENZA*

This essay first appeared as an introduction to Klossowski's translation of Nietzsche's *Die fröhliche Wissenshaft: La Gaya Scienza*, trans. Pierre Klossowski (Paris: Editions du Club Français du Livre, 1956). It is worth noting that Klossowski makes a distinction between the *"gaya scienza,"* Nietzsche's science that considers its objects as aesthetic phenomena, and Nietzsche's book, *"Le Gai Savoir."*

1. In English in the original.

2. Friedrich Nietzsche, *The Gay Science*, trans. Walter Kaufmann (New York: Vintage, 1974), Book 5, §347, p. 340.

3. Klossowski is referring to the translations of *Le Gai Savoir* by Henri Albert (Paris: Mercure de France, 1899), and Alexandre Vialatte (Paris: Gallimard, 1939).

4. *The Gay Science*, Book 5, §377, p. 339.

5. *Genesis* 3:5. In the Garden of Eden, the Serpent tempted Eve with the words "eritis sicut dii": "you will be like gods."

6. Friedrich Nietzsche, "On the Uses and Disadvantages of History for Life," *Untimely Meditations*, trans. R. J. Hollingdale (New York: Cambridge University Press, 1983), §1, p. 61.

7. Ibid.

8. Ibid.

9. Ibid., translation modified.

10. Ibid., §1, p. 62, translation modified.

11. Ibid.

12. "let truth prevail though life perish"; Ibid., §4, p. 78.

13. Ibid., §8, p. 103, translation modified.

14. Ibid., §1, p. 66, translation modified.

15. Ibid., p. 63.

16. A portmanteau word, "*sous-venir*" is coined by Klossowski from the preposition "*sous*," meaning "under" or "beneath" (also used as a prefix usually translated as "sub-"), and the infinitive form of "venir," meaning "to come." It is a homonym of the word "souvenir," both a noun meaning "memory," and a verb meaning "to remember." Finally, it also echoes to a lesser extent the verb "soutenir," meaning "to bear" or "to sustain." It thus carries a sense of remembrance as something that is "undergone," or that one succumbs to.

17. Nietzsche, Letter to Jacob Burckhardt, dated January 6, 1889, in *The Portable Nietzsche*, trans. Walter Kaufmann (New York: Viking Press, 1954), p. 686.

18. *The Gay Science*, Book 5, §343, p. 279, translation modified.

19. Ibid., p. 181, translation modified.

20. The first and final line of Stirner's *The Ego and Its Own*, trans. Steven Byington, ed. David Leopold (Cambridge: Cambridge University Press, 1995); the German phrase is "*Ich hab' mein' Sach' auf Nichts gestellt*," which Byington and Leopold translate as "All things are nothing to me."

21. *The Gay Science*, Book 5, §377, p. 340, translation modified.

22. The final section of *Ecce Homo* is entitled "Why I Am a Destiny." Cf. Friedrich Nietzsche, *The Genealogy of Morals* and *Ecce Homo*, trans. Walter Kaufmann (New York: Vintage, 1990), pp. 326–335.

23. *The Gay Science*, Book 1, §20, p. 92, translation modified.

24. Nietzsche refers to a conference convening all of the European princes in Rome in a letter to August Strindburg, dated December 31, 1888. There are a number of references in Nietzsche's final letters to shooting or "doing away with" one or many anti-Semites. Klossowski probably has in mind the letter to Franz Overbeck, dated January 4, 1889.

25. In a page from his *Journal* dating from 1918, Gide writes "And of course it is possible *after these men* [Socrates, Mahomet, St. Paul, Rousseau, Dostoevsky, Luther] to think as they do without being unbalanced oneself; but it is an unbalanced state that in the beginning brought these thoughts to our rescue, which the reformer needed to re-establish in him the broken equilibrium. It was necessary in fact that, in the beginning, one should be ill to permit, later on, the health of many. Rousseau without his madness would have been only a crude Cicero; and it is precisely in Nietzsche's madness that I see the certificate of his authentic greatness." *André Gide, Journals, Volume 2, 1914–1927*, trans. Justin O'Brien (Chicago: University of Illinois Press, 1948).

26. *The Gay Science*, Book 4, §288, p. 231.

CHAPTER TWO. GIDE, DU BOS, AND THE DEMON

This essay originally appeared in *Les Temps Modernes*, #59, September 1950. Charles Du Bos (1882–1939) was a French literary critic who studied at Oxford and was fluent in both French and English. He wrote criticism as well as being a translator and worked throughout his career to generate interest in English literary works within French intellectual circles. Gide dedicated to Du Bos the account of his religious crisis of 1915–1916, *Numquid et tu . . . ?* [*And you also . . . ?*], which was published in 1922. In it Gide speaks extensively of the demon not merely as a source of temptation, but as a pervasive and active force of persuasion. Du Bos was a close friend and correspondent of Gide's for many years but, following Du Bos's conversion to Catholicism, he published a direct attack upon Gide (*Dialogue avec André Gide*) in 1929. In 1950, Du Bos's *Dialogue avec André Gide* was republished, along with *Lettres de Charles Du Bos et réponses d'André Gide*, and the fourth volume of Du Bos's *Journal intime*, and these three books provided the occasion for Klossowski's essay. A great deal of supplementary material on Du Bos's relation with Gide can be found in the *Journal intime* which chronicles Du Bos's conversion to Catholicism in the 1920s.

1. Literally: "Let Gide perish, and let the devil be." A rephrasing of *"fiat veritas pereat vita,"* "Let there be truth and let life perish."

2. Baudelaire, "My Heart Laid Bare," in *Intimate Journals*, trans. Christopher Isherwood (San Francisco: City Lights, 1990), XLI, p. 63. "There are in every man, two simultaneous postulates [Isherwood renders the French "postulations" as "tendencies"], one to God, the other to Satan. Invocation of God, or Spirituality, is a desire to climb higher; that of Satan, or animality, is delight in descent."

3. Tertullian (ca. 155–230) is one of the most important of the Christian Church Fathers and the first to compose his works in Latin. Tertullian, *On the Soul*, trans. Peter Holmes, *Ante-Nicene Christian Library: Vol XV. The Writings of Tertullian, Vol II* (Edinburgh: T & T Clark, 1870), ch. 57, "Magic and Sorcery Only Apparent in Their Effects. God Alone Can Raise the Dead." "This imposture of the evil spirit lying concealed in the persons of the dead, we are able, if I mistake not, to prove by actual facts, when in cases of exorcism (the evil spirit) affirms himself sometimes to be one of the relatives of the person possessed by him, sometimes a gladiator or a *bestiarius* [beast-fighter], and sometimes even a god; always making it one of his chief cares to extinguish the very truth which we are proclaiming, that men may not readily believe that all souls remove to Hades, and that they may overthrow faith in the resurrection and the judgment."

4. One of the appendices in Gide's *Journal of The Counterfeiters* (appended to the novel) is entitled "Identification of the Demon." In this appendix, which takes the form of a dialogue between two unnamed persons, one of the interlocutors speaks of writing something like a dialogue, entitled "Conversation with the Devil." In the piece, the Devil's first words would be: *"Why should you be afraid of me? You know very well I don't exist."* André Gide, *The Counterfeiters*, trans. Dorothy Bussy (New York: Vintage, 1973), pp. 465–467.

5. Cf. André Gide, *Journals, Volume 3, 1928–1939*, trans. Justin O'Brien (Chicago: University of Illinois Press, 1948), entry dated 12/06/31, p. 206. "As for me, I would rather be vomited than vomit." This is also the final entry from Gide's *Journals* that Mallet includes in *The Correspondence, 1899–1926, Between Paul Claudel and André Gide*.

6. Ibid., entry dated 09/19/29, p. 21, translation modified. Théo Van Rysselberghe (1862–1926) was a Belgian painter who, along with his wife, was a close friend of Gide's.

7. Peter Wust (1884–1940) was a Christian existential philosopher and theologian. He taught at the University of Münster from 1930 until his death from cancer in 1940. Wust went to Paris in 1928, where he met with a number of Catholic thinkers, including Du Bos.

8. Gide's *Dostoïevsky* was first published in 1923.

9. In a conversation on March 2, 1831, Eckermann asked Goethe, "Has not Mephistopheles demonic traits too?" Goethe replied, "No, Mephistopheles is much too negative a being. The Demonic manifests itself in a thoroughly active power." Goethe, *Conversations with Eckermann* (New York: M. Walter Dunne, 1901), pp. 356–357.

10. Cf. *André Gide, Journals, Volume 2, 1914–1927*, trans. Justin O'Brien (Chicago: University of Illinois Press, 1948), undated entry, p. 189, and the appendix "Identification of the Demon" in *Journal of The Counterfeiters*.

CHAPTER THREE. IN THE MARGIN OF THE CORRESPONDENCE BETWEEN GIDE AND CLAUDEL

This essay deals with the correspondence between André Gide and the Catholic author, poet, and diplomat Paul Claudel between 1899 and 1926. This correspondence, together with a number of entries from Gide's *Journal*, were collected and published—with an Introduction and Notes—by Robert Mallet—who had been Gide's secretary for a brief time—in *Correspondance avec Paul Claudel (1899–1926)* (Paris: Gallimard, 1949). In order to maintain continuity with the existing English translation, while preserving the details that Klossowski emphasizes, all translations from Mallet's book have been adapted from *The Correspondence Between Paul Claudel and André Gide*, trans. John Russell (Boston: Beacon Press, 1964). The parenthetical page numbers correspond to the English and French editions, respectively.

1. *André Gide, Journals, Volume 1, 1889–1913*, trans. Justin O'Brien (Chicago: University of Illinois Press, 1947), p. 78, Klossowski's emphasis.

2. Ibid., p. 79.

3. *The Correspondence Between Paul Claudel and André Gide*, letter dated 12/08/05 (48/11).

4. Ibid. (48–49/11–12).

5. Ibid., letter dated 03/19/12 (181/133).

6. Jacques-Bénigne Bossuet (1627–1704) was a French bishop, theologian, and member of the Académie Française. Gide is referring to his work, *History of the Variations of the Protestant Churches*, published in 1688.

7. *André Gide, Journals, Volume 3, 1928–1939*, entry dated 06/26/37, p. 355. This entry was written after Gide and Claudel had broken off their correspondence.

In an interview with Dominique Arban for the journal *Combat*, conducted in March 1947, Claudel is asked about Gide and Gide's puzzlement over this line. Arban's interview is appended to Mallet's book; Claudel's response is found on p. 234.

8. "In order to preserve life, we lose life's meaning." This is a line from Juvenal's *Satires*, VIII, 84. *Theseus* was first published in 1946 by Gallimard.

9. Cf. ibid., journal entry dated 12/05/05 (46/10).

10. *Strait Is the Gate* was first published in 1909 by Mercure de France.

11. Ibid., letter dated 05/10/09 (91/47), Klossowski's emphasis; translation modified.

12. Ibid., letter dated 06/18/09 (92/47), Klossowski's emphasis on "*an admirable mechanism is employed here*," translation modified.

13. Ibid.

14. *André Gide, Journals, Volume 1, 1889–1913*, p. 310, entry dated 01/14/12. Paul-Albert Laurens (1870–1934) was a painter and professor at the École des Beaux-Arts. He was a close friend of Gide's and painted a portrait of the novelist that still hangs in the Luxembourg Museum.

15. Ibid., pp. 311–312, entry dated 01/19/12, translation modified.

16. Ibid., translation modified.

17. Ibid., translation modified.

18. Ibid., letter dated 03/19/12 (180/132), translation modified. Klossowski interjects a note in brackets stating that "the book in question is *The Caves of the Vatican*." Valery Larbaud (1881–1957) was a French writer, novelist, and translator of a number of works including Joyce's *Ulysses*.

19. Ibid. (181/133), translation modified.

20. bid.

21. Ibid., letter to Jacques Rivière dated 03/02/14 (201/156), translation modified.

22. Ibid., letter dated 03/02/14 (202/157), translation modified.

23. Ibid., letter dated 03/07/14 (203/158), Klossowski's emphasis; translation modified.

24. Ibid., letter dated 03/08/14 (204/159), translation modified.

25. Cf. *André Gide, Journals, Volume 1, 1889–1913*, p. 296, from a detached page. Marcel Drouin (1870–1946), who wrote under the pseudonym of Michel Arnauld, was a professor of philosophy and one of the founders of the *N.R.F.*

26. Ibid., letter dated 03/09/14 (207/160), translation modified.

27. Jacques Rivière (1886–1925), a French critic, was an editor at the *N.R.F.* from 1919 until 1925.

28. *The Correspondence Between Paul Claudel and André Gide*, letter dated 03/10/14 (207/160), translation modified.

29. Ibid. (208–209/161–162), translation modified.

30. Klossowski is referring, of course, to the Marquis de Sade.

31. Eugène Montfort (1877–1936) was a French novelist who was involved in the production of the first issue of the *N.R.F.* in 1908, along with Gide. Because of a disagreement between the two, the initial group of editors disbanded and a "new" first issue appeared the following year. The quote cited by Klossowski is from the May 10, 1910, issue of *Les Marges*, a journal founded by Montfort. Gide cites the article, and criticizes it, in his *Journal*.

32. André Gide, *Journals, Volume 1, 1889–1913*, p. 259, entry dated 04/24/10. Justin O'Brien provides a note to his translation indicating that the reference here is "to the story of the beautiful Italian lady who enjoyed the Florentine ices so much that she exclaimed: *"Peccato che non sia una peccata* (What a shame it's not a sin)!" This is a line from the Appendix to *The Counterfeiters* entitled "Identification of the Demon." There may also be a reference here (suggested by the etymological connection of "sorbet" and the Latin verb "sorbeo" which means "to swallow or drink") to "sin-eaters," people who, in exchange for payment, would take upon themselves the sins of someone dying. Typically, the sin-eater would, by means of ritual, transfer the sins first to a piece of food (often bread) and then consume the food and, with it, the dying person's sins. The Catholic Church condemned the practice as a cardinal sin punishable by excommunication. My thanks to Juliana Eimer for pointing out this connection.

33. *The Private Memoirs and Confessions of a Justified Sinner*, James Hogg (Oxford: Oxford University Press, 1999). This novel was originally published in 1824 and tells the story of a young man seduced by the Devil who ends up committing murder. Gide supplied an Introduction for an edition of the book published by the Cresset Press in 1947.

34. André Gide, *Journals, Volume 3, 1928–1939*, p. 7, entry dated 02/27/28, translation modified.

35. Ibid., p. 8.

CHAPTER FOUR. PREFACE TO
A MARRIED PRIEST BY BARBEY D'AUREVILLY

This essay first appeared as a Preface to *Un prêtre marié* by Barbey d'Aurevilly, (Éditions du Club Français du Livre, Paris, 1960). Jules Amédée Barbey d'Aurevilly (1808–1889) was a French novelist who is now perhaps best known for his collection of stories *Les Diaboliques* [*The She-Devils*] as well as his extreme and eccentric Catholicism and dandyism.

1. Thomas de Quincey (1785–1859) was an English author, most famous perhaps for his *Confessions of an English Opium-Eater*, first published in 1822, from which this quote is taken.

2. Jean-Paul Marat (1743–1793) was identified with the Jacobin faction during the French Revolution and was instrumental in the creation of the Reign of Terror. He was murdered in his bathtub (where he sought frequent relief from a skin disease) by Charlotte Corday, a member of the Girondins (a rival Revolutionary group).

Alphonse Marie Louise Prat de Lamartine (1790–1869) was a prominent poet and politician in France, elected to the Académie Française in 1822, who was also the author of a two-volume history of the Girondins [*Histoire des Girondins* (Paris: Furne, 1847)]. During the Revolution of 1848, Lamartine was briefly the head of the government. Following this, he assumed the position of Minister of Foreign Affairs, before retiring from political life and devoting himself to literature. Lamartine was a pantheist and an important influence on the French Symbolist poets.

3. *nihil obstat*: "nothing stands in the way." This is the stamp of the Catholic censor, to whom manuscripts are submitted by authors seeking approval for their works. If they receive this stamp, their works are sent on to the bishop, who then decides whether they will be published.

4. A "fin de non-reçevoir" is a legal exception or plea that shows the plaintiff has no right to bring the charge either because a certain time period has expired, or because there has been some event that has vitiated the original cause for action.

5. *La Chouannerie* was the name of a royalist guerrilla movement active in Brittany at various times in the late eighteenth and early nineteenth centuries.

6. Joseph de Maistre (1753–1821) was a prominent conservative philosopher and politician. Following the Revolution of 1789, de Maistre argued for the return of the divinely sanctioned monarchy.

7. *Lettres à Trébutien* (Paris: François Bernouard, 1927), v. 3, pp. 215–216, letter dated March 14, 1855.

8. *Le Chevalier des Touches* [*The Knight of Touches*], first published in 1864. In addition to "bellows," "*soufflets*" can also mean (physical) "blows," and "*touches*" may be rendered as "touches" (as with a brush).

9. Cymodocée is the name of one of the main characters in Chateaubriand's *Les Martyrs* (1809). Raised as a pagan in Greece during the reign of the Roman Emperor Diocletian, she is destined by God to marry the Christian Eudorus. After their marriage, the new emperor, Galerius, issues a decree condemning all Christians. Returning to Rome to defend other Christians, Eudorus is arrested and, when she refuses to renounce Christianity, Cymodocée joins her husband in the Coliseum where they are devoured. The name comes from a Nereid and, literally, means "wave-receiver." She is mentioned in passing by Hesiod; she is one of the Nereids who go with Thetis to console her son Achilles after he hears of the death of Patroclus in Book 18 of *The Iliad*; she appears twice in *The Aeneid*, once in Book 5 as one of a group of Nereids accompanying Neptune, and again, prominently, in Book 10 where she speaks with Aeneas (as the Nereid who knows human speech the best) and urges him on to fight Turnus.

10. George Bernanos (1888–1948) was a Catholic French writer best known, perhaps, for his *The Diary of a Country Priest* (1936), which was adapted and made into a movie by Robert Bresson in 1950.

11. Marquis de Sade, *Eugénie de Franval* (Paris: Les Editions Georges Artigues, 1948); translated into English as *Incest*, trans. Andrew Brown (London: Hesperus Press, 2003).

12. *Lettres à Trébutien*, v. 3, p. 285, letter dated June 28, 1855.

CHAPTER FIVE. THE MASS OF GEORGES BATAILLE

This essay originally appeared in *84*, in September 1950.

1. The reference here is to the theologian and mystic, Meister Eckhart (circa 1260–1328).

CHAPTER SIX. LANGUAGE, SILENCE, AND COMMUNISM

This essay originally appeared in *Critique* (with the subtitle "On *L'Embarras du choix* [*The Trouble with Choice*], by Brice Parain") in June 1949. Brice Parain (1897–1971) was a prominent philosopher and theologian in France for much of the twentieth century who wrote extensively on problems of language.

1. Tertullian (ca. 155–230) is one of the most important of the Christian Church Fathers. His principal work concerning the heresy of the Docetes is *De Carne Christi* (*On the Body of Christ*). The Docetes (Gnostics) believed in the divinity of Christ but not in the ability of God to assume material form. For them, Christ was not material at all, but merely a sort of phantasm produced by the Divine.

2. Ibid., p. 119.

3. *L'Embarras du choix*, p. 80.

4. Ibid., p. 81.

5. Ibid., p. 84.

6. Ibid.

7. Cf. Søren Kierkegaard, *The Concept of Anxiety*, ed. and trans. Reidar Thomte and Albert B. Anderson (Princeton: Princeton University Press, 1980), "Anxiety about the Good (The Demonic)," pp. 118–154. Parain refers specifically to Kierkegaard's discussion of the demonic on p. 87 of *L'Embarras du choix*, calling it, in a footnote, "the fundamental category of the dialectic."

8. *L'Embarras du choix*, p. 88.

9. Ibid., p. 86, note 2.

10. Ibid., p. 87

11. Cf. *L'Embarras du choix*, p. 92

12. Cf. *L'Embarras du choix*, p. 93

13. Ibid.

14. Ibid., pp. 93–94.

15. *L'Embarras du choix*, pp. 94–95. Leibniz's argument can be found in "Meditations on Knowledge, Truth, and Ideas," in *Philosophical Essays*, trans. Garber and Ariew (Indianapolis: Hackett, 1989), p. 25.

16. *L'Embarras du choix*, p. 94, note 1.

17. Klossowski's text reads, "Tous les noms demandent à être le plus commun comme le plus noble de l'existence." Parain's text, which Klossowski is following,

reads, "Tous les noms demandent à être, le plus commun comme le plus noble" (*L'Embarras du Choix*, p. 95). It seems likely that there should be a comma in Klossowski's text after "être," and the translation reflects this. Without the comma, the sentence would read: "Every name asks to be the most common as well as the most noble name of existence."

18. "Aller et Retour," p. 234.

19. *L'Embarras du Choix*, XIV, pp. 134–164.

20. Ibid., p. 135.

21. Ibid., p. 138.

22. Ibid., p. 139.

23. Ibid., p. 140.

24. Ibid., p. 141.

25. Ibid.

26. Ibid., p. 143.

27. Ibid., p. 148.

28. Ibid., p. 150.

29. Ibid.

30. Ibid., p. 151.

31. Ibid., p. 160.

32. Ibid., p. 162—following Parain's text by substituting "parole" for "part."

33. Ibid., p. 164.

CHAPTER SEVEN. ON MAURICE BLANCHOT

As Klossowski's first note indicates, this essay was previously published in *Les Temps Modernes* where it carried the subtitle "On Maurice Blanchot's *Death Sentence* and *The Most High*." In order to maintain continuity with the existing English translation, while preserving the details that Klossowski emphasizes, all translations from *The Most High* have been adapted from Allan Stoekl's English translation (Lincoln: University of Nebraska Press, 1996). When Klossowski makes reference to specific page numbers in the body of the essay, those numbers have been changed to correspond to the English translation and the relevant pages in the original French edition have been indicated in the endnotes (or in square brackets when the citation is itself in a note). When no reference is given in Klossowski's text, references have been provided to both the English and the French editions, with the English given first, the French second.

1. Tertullian, *On the Resurrection of the Flesh*, trans. Peter Holmes, *Ante-Nicene Christian Library: Vol XV. The Writings of Tertullian, Vol II* (Edinburgh: T&T Clark, 1870), ch. 30 "This Vision Interpreted by Tertullian of the Resurrection of the Bodies of the Dead. A Chronological Error of Our Author, Who Supposes that Ezekiel in

His Ch. XXXI. Prophesied Before the Captivity." "Now, although there is a sketch of
the true thing in its image, the image itself still possesses a truth of its own: it must
needs be, therefore, that must have a prior existence for itself, which is used figuratively to express some other thing. Vacuity is not a consistent basis for a similitude,
nor does nonentity form a suitable foundation for a parable."

2. Maurice Blanchot, "Literature and the Right to Death," in *The Work of Fire*,
trans. Charlotte Mandell (Stanford: Stanford University Press, 1995), pp. 324ff.

3. This phrase operates as a sort of refrain in Blanchot's essay "Literature and
the Right to Death," pp. 322, 327, 336. Mandell renders it as "the life that endures
death and maintains itself in it."

4. The French text of this sentence reads: "*Or, le sens, s'il n'est possible qu'à partir d'un commencement et dans la perspective d'une fin, n'est pas sens s'il ne demeure dans
l'existant en devenir se désavouant sans cesse en tant que monde ce contexte de vicissitudes
que l'on nomme l'histoire.*"

5. A portmanteau word, "*sous-vient*" is coined by Klossowski from the preposition "*sous*," meaning "under" or "beneath" (also used as a prefix usually translated as
"sub-"), and the third-person present, indicative form of "*venir*," meaning "to come."
It is a homonym of the word "*souvenir*," both a noun meaning "memory," and a verb
meaning "to remember." Finally, it also echoes to a lesser extent the verb "*soutenir*,"
meaning "to bear" or "to sustain." It thus carries a sense of remembrance as something
that is "undergone" or that one succumbs to.

6. Maurice Blanchot, *The Most High* (9/1).

7. Ibid. (57–58).

8. Ibid. (237–238).

9. Ibid. (71/74).

10. Blanchot, "Literature and the Right to Death," p. 327.

11. Blanchot, "Literature and the Right to Death," pp. 328–330.

12. Blanchot, *The Most High* (176/171).

13. "A dialectical solecism of God." A solecism is a syntactical error.

14. Blanchot, *The Most High* (54/58).

15. Ibid. (231/222), Klossowski's emphasis.

16. Ibid. (231/222).

17. Ibid. (231/222).

18. Ibid. (224/233).

19. Ibid. (72/75).

20. Ibid. (241/230).

21. Ibid. (242/231).

22. Ibid. (242/231–232).

23. Ibid. (244/234).

24. Ibid. (246/235).

25. Ibid. (253–254/243).

CHAPTER EIGHT. NIETZSCHE, POLYTHEISM, AND PARODY

This is a slightly revised version of a translation that appeared in the *Bulletin for the Société Américaine de Philosophie de Langue Française*, Vol. 14, No. 2, Fall 2004.

1. Klossowski is referring to the work of Charles Andler, *Nietzsche, sa vie et sa pensée*, 3 vols. (Paris: Gallimard, 1958).

2. "Let there be truth and let life perish." Friedrich Nietzsche, *Untimely Meditations*, trans. R. J. Hollingdale (New York: Cambridge University Press, 1983), §4, p. 78.

3. "What an artist perishes with me." These are the last words attributed to the Roman emperor Nero. Nietzsche quotes them in *The Gay Science*, trans. Walter Kaufmann (New York: Vintage, 1974), Book 1, §36, p. 105.

4. Friedrich Nietzsche, *Ecce Homo*, in *Basic Writings of Nietzsche*, ed. and trans. Walter Kaufmann (New York: Modern Library, 1992), "Thus Spoke Zarathustra: A Book for All and None," §5, p. 759.

5. Friedrich Nietzsche, *Twilight of the Idols*, trans. Walter Kaufmann, in *The Portable Nietzsche* (New York: Viking Press, 1954), pp. 485–486.

6. A portmanteau word, "sous-vient" is coined by Klossowski from the preposition "*sous*," meaning "under" or "beneath" (also used as a prefix usually translated as "sub-"), and the third-person present, indicative form of "*venir*," meaning "to come." "*Sous-vient*" also echoes the word "*souvenir*," both a noun meaning "memory," and a verb meaning "to remember." Finally, it also echoes, though to a lesser extent, the verb "*soutenir*," meaning "to bear" or "to sustain." It thus carries a sense of remembrance as something that is "undergone" or that one succumbs to (an inactivity of consciousness preparatory for the coming forth [*advient*, in the next sentence] of the past).

7. Friedrich Nietzsche, *Thus Spoke Zarathustra*, in *The Portable Nietzsche* (New York: Viking Press, 1954), Second Part, "On Redemption," p. 253.

8. Nietzsche, *Gay Science*, Book 3, §112, p. 172.

9. Ibid., §111, pp. 171–172.

10. Ibid., §110, pp. 169–171.

11. Ibid.

12. Ibid.

13. *Ephesians* 5:13.

14. *Ephesians* 5:11.

15. *John I* 1:5.

16. Nietzsche, *Gay Science*, Book 5, §354, pp. 297–300.

17. Ibid.

18. "Dépense" means, literally, "expenditure," or "waste"; the verb "*dépenser*" means "to spend" and can also mean "to consume." It occurs frequently in the work of Bataille, where it is usually translated into English as "expenditure." Klossowski uses it to express the nongoal-oriented expenditure of unconscious impulses; incommunicable pathos. The contrast between this exertion and that of thinking can be seen in the components of the word itself: "de-," a preposition that can have the sense of negation (as in "*démonter*," "to dis-mount"), and "*pense*," the imperative form of the verb "penser," "to think." The word thus also carries a sense of "to unthink."

19. Friedrich Nietzsche, *The Will to Power*, ed. Walter Kaufmann, trans. Walter Kaufmann and R. J. Hollingdale (New York: Vintage Books, 1967), Book 3, Section 4, §493 [1885], p. 272.

20. Nietzsche, *Gay Science*, Preface to the Second Edition, §1, p. 33, translation modified.

21. Nietzsche, *Gay Science*, §1, pp. 74–76.

22. See Nietzsche, *Will to Power*, Book 3, Section IV, §853, "Art in *The Birth of Tragedy*," p. 451.

23. Zarathustra first encounters the Last Pope in *Thus Spoke Zarathustra*, Fourth Part, §6, "Retired," pp. 370–375.

24. Nietzsche, *Gay Science*, Book 5, §361, pp. 316–317.

25. Nietzsche, *Ecce Homo*, "Why I Am a Destiny," §9, in *Basic Writings of Nietzsche*, p. 791.

26. Karl Löwith, *Nietzsche's Philosophy of the Eternal Return of the Same*, trans. J. Harvey Lomax (Berkeley: University of California Press, 1997).

27. Nietzsche, letter to Jacob Burckhardt, dated January 6, 1889, in *The Portable Nietzsche*, p. 686.

28. Ibid, p. 685.

29. Nietzsche, *Thus Spoke Zarathustra*, Third Part, "On Old and New Tablets," p. 309.

30. Nietzsche, *Gay Science*, Book 5, §346, pp. 285–287.

31. Ibid., §370, pp. 327–331.

32. Nietzsche, *Thus Spoke Zarathustra*, Second Part, "Upon the Blessed Isles," p. 199, translation modified.

33. Nietzsche, *Thus Spoke Zarathustra*, Third Part, "On Apostates," p. 294.

34. Of or relating to the pagan Isis cults.

35. Nietzsche, *Thus Spoke Zarathustra*, Fourth Part, "The Ass Festival," p. 426, translation modified.

TRANSLATOR'S AFTERWORD: KLOSSOWSKI'S *SALTO MORTALE*

1. In the Introduction to his translation of Virgil's *Aeneid*, Klossowski writes, "The dislocated aspect of the syntax . . . should not be treated as some arbitrary pell-mell, able to be readjusted according to our own grammatical logic, in the translation of a poem where it is precisely the voluntary juxtaposition of words (whose shock produces the sonorous richness and the magic [*prestige*] of the image) that constitutes the physiognomy of each verse . . . Virgil's epic poem is in effect a theater where words *mime* the characters' gestures and states of soul, just as by their arrangement they also mime the proper accompaniments of the action. The words, not bodies, are what take on a disposition [attitude]; they are what is woven, not the clothing; they scintillate, not the armor; they howl, not the storm." Cited by Alain Arnaud in *Pierre Klossowski* (Paris: Éditions du Seuil, 1990), p. 19.

2. Virgil, *Aeneid*, Book VI, line 721.

3. Cf. Plato, *Apology*, trans. G. M. A. Grube, in *Plato: Complete Works*, ed. John M. Cooper (Indianapolis: Hackett, 1997), p. 29 (31c–32a). On the etymology of the terms, see the relevant entries in A. G. Liddell and R. Scott, *Greek-English Lexicon with a Revised Supplement*, 9th ed. by Stuart Jones and McKenzie (New York: Clarendon / Oxford University Press, 1996).

4. Klosswski's notion of subcoming is echoed by Deleuze's reading of Proust's involuntary memory. "The Search for lost time is in fact a search for truth. . . . Proust does not believe that man, nor even a supposedly pure mind, has by nature a desire for truth, a will-to-truth. We search for truth only when we are determined to do so in terms of a concrete situation, when we undergo a kind of violence that impels us to such a search." Gilles Deleuze, *Proust & Signs: The Complete Text*, trans. Richard Howard (Minneapolis: University of Minnesota Press, 2000).

5. "Celestial" here is meant to echo Anchises' description of the "caelestis origo" of the energy that directs primordial spirit. Virgil, *Aeneid*, Book VI., line 730.

6. Friedrich Nietzsche, *Ecce Homo*, in *Basic Writings of Nietzsche*, ed. and trans. Walter Kaufmann (New York: Modern Library, 1992), "Thus Spoke Zarathustra: A Book for All and None," §1, p. 752.

7. Cf. "And to the extent that knowledge thereby develops the power of metamorphosis, a life lived once and for all suddenly appears more impoverished than a single instant rich with many ways of existing; this is why a single instant thus charged, thus subcomed to [*sous-venu*] in the suspension of the consciousness of the present, suffices to reverse the course of a life. Hence the illuminative character of the *Gaya Scienza* whose many aphorisms testify to the moments of an ecstatic serenity: because from then on he had the feeling (formulated seven years later at the height of his madness) *that at bottom I am every name in history*, of losing his own identity in the very certitude of finding it again, multiplied, in the identical permanence of the universe." "On Some Fundamental Themes of Nietzsche's *Gaya Scienza*," p. 12.

8. In "La synthèse disjunctive," an extract from *Anti-Oedipus* that they contributed to an issue of *L'Arc* devoted to Klossowski, Deleuze, and Guattari attribute to

Klossowski the "double articulation" that regards the body and mind as reflecting one another. Gilles Deleuze and Félix Guattari, "La synthèse disjunctive," in *L'Arc* 43, Klossowski (1970), pp. 54–62.

9. This novel also appears in English under the title *Lafcadio's Adventures*.

10. "In the Margin of the Correspondence Between Gide and Claudel," p. 68. The "fungibility of souls" is a chief concern in Klossowski's *La monnaie vivante* (Paris: Terrain Vague, 1970).

11. "According to Gide the Devil is an agent of redoubling. This is well known to Gide thanks to the Other having borrowed, in its nonexistence, the existence of a Claudel, of a Charles Du Bos." "Gide, Du Bos, and the Demon," p. 42.

12. "This is precisely what constitutes the interest of one aspect of this singular book: the structure of the human soul is made such that it would not know how to act without prohibition, nor could it be constituted without it: in order to sustain itself, the adherence to atheism resuscitates all the prohibitions that belief is based on— from then on it must fortify itself against its return." "Preface to *A Married Priest* by Barbey d'Aurevilly," p. 81.

13. "Nietzsche, Polytheism, and Parody," p. 165.

14. Ibid., p. 168.

15. Ibid., p. 169.

16. Ibid., p. 170.

Index

147